Agile Faculty

# Agile

# Faculty

Practical Strategies for
Managing Research,
Service, and Teaching

REBECCA POPE-RUARK

The University of Chicago Press

Chicago and London

The University of Chicago Press, Chicago 60637
The University of Chicago Press, Ltd., London
© 2017 by The University of Chicago
All rights reserved. No part of this book may be used or reproduced in any manner
whatsoever without written permission, except in the case of brief quotations in
critical articles and reviews. For more information, contact the University of Chicago
Press, 1427 E. 60th St., Chicago, IL 60637.
Published 2017
Printed in the United States of America

26  25  24  23  22  21  20  19  18  17       1  2  3  4  5

ISBN-13: 978-0-226-46301-8 (cloth)
ISBN-13: 978-0-226-46315-5 (paper)
ISBN-13: 978-0-226-46329-2 (e-book)
DOI: 10.7208/chicago/9780226463292.001.0001

Library of Congress Cataloging-in-Publication Data

Names: Pope-Ruark, Rebecca, author.
Title: Agile faculty : practical strategies for managing research, service, and
    teaching / Rebecca Pope-Ruark.
Description: Chicago ; London : The University of Chicago Press, 2017. | Includes
    bibliographical references.
Identifiers: LCCN 2017024539 | ISBN 9780226463018 (cloth : alk. paper) | ISBN
    9780226463155 (pbk. : alk. paper) | ISBN 9780226463292 (e-book)
Subjects: LCSH: College teaching. | Universities and colleges—Faculty. | Project
    management. | Agile software development. | Scrum (Computer software
    development)
Classification: LCC LB2331.P577 2017 | DDC 378.1/25—dc23
LC record available at https://lccn.loc.gov/2017024539

♾ This paper meets the requirements of ANSI/NISO Z39.48-1992 (Permanence
of Paper).

# Contents

*Acknowledgments*   xi

*Author's Note*   xiii

**1   Reimagining Paths to Faculty Vitality in Higher Education**   *1*

Understanding Faculty Career Stresses   *4*

New Faculty

Mid-career Faculty

Women Faculty

Faculty of Color

Contingent Faculty

Shifting the Narrative   *8*

Introducing Agile and Scrum   *10*

Origins of Agile and Scrum

Scrum Values

Applying Agile to Faculty Work   *16*

An Agile Faculty Manifesto

Agile Faculty Values

Enacting the Agile Faculty Mindset   *20*

**2    Working the Agile Way Using Scrum**  *23*

What Is Scrum?  *25*

How Is Scrum Different?

What Is the Scrum Process?

What Happens during the Sprint?

How Have I Used Scrum in My Own Experience?  *33*

A Research Example

A Service Example

A Teaching Example

Wrapping Up  *39*


**3    Organizing and Prioritizing Your Personal Research Agenda**  *41*

To-Do List vs. Backlog  *42*

Create Your Research Agenda Backlog  *45*

Build a Realistic Sprint Plan from the Backlog  *49*

Make Your Sprint Backlog Visible  *51*

Remain Agile in the Face of Change or Opportunity  *55*

Wrapping Up  *56*


**4    Running a Collaborative Research Project or Program**  57

Understanding the Foundations of Collaboration  *59*

Laying the Groundwork for Good Scrum Research Teams  *62*

Who, and How Many?

How Will You Work Together?

Prioritizing, Estimating, and Visualizing the Research Backlog  *67*

Prioritizing with a Product Owner

Estimating Backlog Stories

*Estimating with T-shirt Sizing*

*Estimating with Story Points*

Estimating in Practice

Scaling the Backlog across Multiple Teams    *72*

Wrapping Up    *76*


**5    Leading Effective Agile Committees    77**

Serving as an Agile Leader    *79*

Launching (or Resetting) the Agile Faculty Committee    *80*

Pick the Right People

Hold a Committee Retreat

*Team Building*

*Committee Charter Development*

*Goal Setting and Backlog Generating*

*First Sprint Planning*

Facilitating the Agile Committee    *90*

Setting Meeting Agendas

Facilitating Discussion

Managing Conflict

Wrapping Up    *95*


**6    Mentoring Students and Peers with Agile Activities    97**

Understanding Mentorship as an Agile Teaching Activity    *98*

Using Epics and Stories with Undergraduate Mentees    *100*

Mentoring Research Students    *104*

Mentoring New Faculty    *108*

Mutual Faculty Mentoring    *113*

Wrapping Up    *118*


**7    Organizing Your Course as an Epic    *119***

Rethinking Backward Design as Agile Course Design    *121*

Brainstorming about the Course

Articulating Epics and Stories

Determining Assessment Criteria for Epics

Framing the Course Schedule

Creating a New Course Using Agile Backward Design   *132*

Grant Writing: Brainstorming about the Course

Grant Writing: Articulating Epics and Stories

Grant Writing: Determining Assessment Criteria for Epics

Grant Writing: Framing the Course Schedule

Revising an Existing Course Using Agile Backward Design   *137*

Publishing: Brainstorming about the Course

Publishing: Articulating Epics and Stories

Publishing: Determining Assessment Criteria for Epics

Publishing: Framing the Course Schedule

Adapting the Agile Backward Design Process in Other Contexts   *144*

Multi-section Courses

Curriculum (Re)Design

Wrapping Up   *146*

Appendix 7.1: Complete Schedule for Grant Writing Course   *147*

Appendix 7.2: Complete Schedule for Publishing   *148*

**8    Planning and Implementing Scrum-Based Group Projects**   *149*

Comparing Cooperation and Collaboration   *151*

Aligning a Group Project Idea with Important Course Considerations   *152*

Creating a Short Group Project with One Sprint   *155*

Creating a Long Group Project with Multiple Sprints   *160*

Writing the Assignment Sheet   *166*

Encouraging Collaboration and Introducing Scrum   *168*

Acting as Product Owner and Scrum Master   *171*

Product Owner

Scrum Master

Wrapping Up   *174*

## Afterword: Imagining the Agile College and University  *175*

What if . . .  *176*

> . . . important committees ran like Scrum teams?
>
> . . . student and faculty peer mentoring used an Agile coaching approach?
>
> . . . programs were sprint- rather than semester-based?
>
> . . . research teams were housed in interdisciplinary, collaborative, Agile centers?
>
> . . . academic publishing used an Agile model?

Wrapping Up  *181*

*References*  *183*

# Acknowledgments

This project would not have been possible without extensive support from Elon University and Elon's Center for the Advancement of Teaching and Learning (CATL), Peter Felten, in particular.

My Professional Writing and Rhetoric colleagues Jessie Moore, Paula Rosinski, Michael Strickland, Li Li, and Tim Peeples, as well as friends Jennifer Veltsos, Ashley Patriarca, and Matthew Search, provided much needed feedback and encouragement throughout the writing process, for which I am deeply grateful.

I thank the anonymous peer reviewers of this manuscript for their detailed feedback; the text is all the better for their insights.

I'd also like to thank my former student Caitlin Rantala for designing the Scrum process graphic I have been using for several years now and which appears in this volume as figures 1.2 and 2.2.

Last but certainly not least, I thank my family for their support and my husband Tracey for introducing me to Scrum, debating the finer points of stories and roles, and being my biggest cheerleader.

# Author's Note

Thank you for taking the time to read this book, a passion project of mine over the past few years. Faculty professional development is crucial to our ability to address change, consider new ideas, and achieve goals in our academic careers.

An interest in helping students collaborate more effectively has taken me on a compelling journey over the past nine years, and I'm happy to share some of my findings and hypotheses with you here. Agile is still young as a work and productivity philosophy, the first set of values and processes having been fully codified in 2001. Advocates of Agile face an uphill battle against what social innovator Zaid Hassan (2014) calls "the culturally dominant technocratic approach" with its deeply entrenched focus on time-consuming planning, linear project stages, and command-and-control leadership styles (p. 21). Agile strategies are the polar opposite of this, founded in the principles of design thinking and focused on iterative planning, collaborative progress toward goals, and distributed expertise. As a faculty member, I have found that the Agile process and the Agile values of focus, courage, openness, commitment, and respect echo my own philosophy. Using these strategies, I have personally become more engaged in my work, more productive, and more excited about reaching my long-term professional goals.

But because Agile is young, thorough empirical research on its effectiveness is still in progress in industry. Literature on Agile's effectiveness in the software development industry, where it began, can be found in computing sciences and management journals. To date, very few people outside of computing sciences and management seem to be writing about Agile academically. I have found little, if any, literature on Agile in higher education broadly except for my own work combining Agile and Scholarship of Teaching and Learning (SoTL). For these reasons, this text does not rely on published or empirical academic research to support my claims of Agile's usefulness in faculty work. Instead, I draw from personal experience, reasonable hypotheses, and the rich information available on trusted industry blogs, online news magazines, and process texts published by respected presses.

Many examples in this text come from my own years of experience adapting Agile strategies in my classroom, research, and consulting. But some of the examples are hypothetical. These strategies have been proven to work across different industries but are making much slower inroads into higher education practices. I believe they can work in contexts such as faculty committees and mentoring relationships. But I have yet to see research or blog posts that report on Agile being used in these ways. In a true Agile spirit, please try the strategies in the book, and let me know how they worked for you. I hope to replace the examples from my experience and the hypothetical situations with your experiences, making the book itself iterative and Agile.

Most of the examples in this text are also somewhat simplified. Faculty life is complex. And the complexities vary across different types of institutions, roles and appointments, personal and professional commitments, family and personal responsibilities, etc. I recognize that and value it. But the examples are simple because the strategies themselves are simple. They can be adapted in many ways in many different contexts. I purposely chose not to overcomplicate the examples, fearing this might discourage creative thinking about how you can adapt Agile in your unique context.

Again, I hope that you will adapt the strategies and share with me so that we can include your adaptations as examples or case studies in future iterations of this book. Did the committee strategies work? Do you have advice for leading a complex research team after implementing Scrum? What advice do you have for using any of the strategies in faculty development roles? Please share with me at rruark@elon.edu.

In this text, I take the perspective that we are colleagues, and I'm writing to you directly. As such, the tone is less formal than that of a standard academic piece and is reflected in several strategic language choices throughout. If I use the pronoun *you*, I'm talking to you as a colleague and fellow faculty member. If I use *we*, I'm including myself in that circle. I hope that the text will remind you of a professional development workshop rather than a stuffy lecture on strategies that should be applied rather than preached.

Finally, I advise you to be Agile when approaching the text. *Agile Faculty* is practical and not meant to be read linearly. Even I can admit that the book is quite boring when read that way. Instead, read the first two chapters for context and an overview of the Agile framework Scrum, then read whatever chapter interests you. Try out the strategies, adapt them, report back, then try another chapter. It is my hope that you will find the Agile mindset and Scrum process useful to your faculty work in diverse ways. Agile is about making continuous, iterative progress toward big goals, and in many ways progress *is* the goal. One of the creators of the Scrum process, Jeff Sutherland (2014), argues, "Work . . . can flow; it can be an expression of joy, an alignment toward a higher purpose. We can be better. We can be great! We just have to practice" (p. 39). Happy practicing!

# 1

# Reimagining Paths to Faculty Vitality in Higher Education

A new faculty member at a selective liberal arts college looks for ways to balance teaching, research, and service requirements while adjusting to life at a rural land-grant institution after completing his PhD at an urban campus. In another department, a part-time, non-tenure-track faculty member enjoys teaching at two very different universities but continues a frustrating search for a permanent position in the area because his partner has a good, stable job locally.

A pre-tenure faculty member at a large research-extensive university works to manage a large lab, write grants to fund the lab, mentor graduate students, and keep up with her teaching load, which sometimes interferes with her family life. At the same institution, a tenured faculty member strives to juggle her two children and aging parents, while exploring the possibility of starting a new research agenda or moving into administration to fend off mid-career malaise.

A recently tenured computing sciences faculty member from an underrepresented group at a research-intensive college diligently

1

integrates his time teaching two classes per semester with a new Scholarship of Teaching and Learning (SoTL) research agenda while fielding frequent requests to serve on diversity and inclusion committees and mentor minority students. At the same time, a faculty member at a community college with a heavy teaching and service load has many ideas for SoTL research in her classes but not enough time to write up the IRB proposal and conduct the studies.

Many things attract individual faculty members to the academic path, and perhaps like the monastic life it was originally patterned after, it appeals to a set of personal and professional values unique to those who choose it. Some are called to generate and contribute new knowledge for the betterment of society through research, others to support the next generation of our citizens through excellent teaching, and others yet to give service for the improvement of social structures and communities, while some to do all three with equal passion. These motivations reflect the ideal in American higher education of the "complete faculty member," who is the ultimate teacher-scholar, highly productive in all areas of academic work (Fairweather, 2002, p. 28).

Faculty life can be complex, overwhelming, empowering, and dynamic. And faculty life is constantly changing; higher education is regularly transformed by the political, intellectual, and economic climate in which we live and work. As the media and government call for greater productivity, usually in terms of research output and credit hours taught, faculty agency to direct teaching, research, and service activities may seem more limited than autonomy-craving academics might like. As such, each faculty member introduced in the opening vignettes strives for that complete faculty member ideal while facing unique challenges and opportunities based on a number of factors: type of institution, type of appointment, career stage, gender, race, family situation, and personal commitment to teaching, research, and/or service.

Success in each of these environments will look very different as definitions of faculty agency and productivity continue to evolve in these contexts. Author Susan Robison (2013) argues that faculty often function more like entrepreneurs and, as such, make decision after decision every day about how to spend time, achieve goals, and meet self-imposed high standards of performance (pp. 3, 11). These daily micro-decisions can be overwhelming and potentially overshadow higher order professional goals. Higher education researcher Roger Baldwin (1990) found that "vital faculty," those faculty who maintain engagement and passion over the course of a long career, have clearly articulated and concrete short-term and long-term goals that guide work in all aspects of their careers; they take more risks and actively look for professional growth opportunities, which leads to more fluid, multidimensional careers over time (pp. 172, 174). He and his colleagues also found that a lack of these concrete goals can "lead to a loss of professional momentum or even disengagement," specifically among mid-career and senior faculty who have already achieved tenure and promotion (Baldwin et al., 2008, p. 52). Similarly Dankowski and colleagues (2009) argue that vitality comes from a strong connection between "satisfaction, productivity, and engagement" that enables faculty members to realize personal and institutional goals (summarized in Palmer et al., 2011, p. 21).

How do faculty achieve this level of professional agency, autonomy, and achievement in the changing landscape of higher education? What frameworks exist for helping faculty to not only clearly articulate goals but also make consistent, measured progress even as contexts shift? Many faculty have priority management systems that work for them individually, and useful popular systems exist for managing time and productivity, ranging from the Getting Things Done method and Pomodoro Technique to the strategy Robison outlines in *Peak Performing Faculty*. In this book, I argue that a relatively new framework that is taking many industries by storm, Agile, can also be applied alone or in conjunction with other systems to achieve meaningful personal and professional goals.

This book looks at how academic professionals can draw on the values and practices of the Agile movement to become what I call "Agile faculty." Agile represents a sea change in management philosophy, moving away from Frederick Taylor's 19th-century ideals of scientific management to a more purpose-based, people-driven, learning-focused approach to achieving clearly articulated goals. Based on a combination of transparent commitment to specific goals and incremental but controlled progress toward them, Agile frameworks, such as Scrum, provide an empirical process to accomplish meaningful work while supporting responsiveness to change (Hartman, 2012, pp. 11.5, 11.7). I have been using Agile practices in all aspects of my faculty activities for more than nine years and teaching these strategies to colleagues and students for eight. While certainly not a cure-all for faculty stress or contextual challenges, I firmly believe these approaches can support faculty members' journeys of professional vitality and also potentially transform some of the underlying functions of higher education.

In this book, you'll learn more about the Agile perspective, the Scrum framework, and strategies you can immediately implement in your research, service, and teaching activities to achieve your most significant goals. This introductory chapter explores what I mean when I say "Agile faculty" and the mindset associated with becoming such. First, I review some of the challenges facing faculty like those in the introductory vignettes, exploring just a sampling of the literature on faculty work-life and stress to provide context for why an Agile mindset can be beneficial. I then shift gears to delve into scholarship on faculty vitality and productivity, which can inform one's quest for sustained professional growth and satisfaction. Finally, I make the clear connections between this research and Agile, explaining its roots and goals and then outlining what an Agile faculty approach might look like, in preparation for the practical strategies offered in the rest of the book.

## Understanding Faculty Career Stresses

Faculty today face many contextual challenges that affect how we approach research, service, and teaching responsibilities as well as work-life integration. Since the 1990s, faculty work has been called into question by government representatives and the general public, as the image of the tenured professor in a cushy office doing very little work for too much pay pervades (Johnsrud, 2008; O'Meara, Terosky & Neumann, 2009; Rosenthal et al., 1994). Calls for accountability, productivity, and transparency from these constituencies have led to dramatic changes in higher education and in faculty workloads. Most recently, for example, the Obama administration unveiled the College Scorecard in 2013, sorting US institutions by costs, graduation rate, loan default rate, average amount borrowed, and employment to help families make more economical decisions about the costs of higher education (US Department of Education). Conservative leaders in states like North Carolina push for more career-training programs in their public universities. For-profit universities such as Corinthian Colleges and private institutions like Sweet Briar College made the news in 2015 for unexpected closures, though Sweet Briar did earn a reprieve. Budget cuts at public institutions, endowment concerns at private institutions, and increasing tuition prices are affecting program offerings and enrollment numbers all over the United States.

Research on faculty stress points toward factors such as time constraints; concerns about tenure, promotion, and recognition; home and family concerns; student contact; and unclear professional identity as sources of stress (e.g., Day, 1994; Gmelch, Wilke & Lovrich, 1986; Hendel & Horn, 2008), all of which are "mediated by the institutional context, which may differ by mission, available resources, and collegiality" (Hendel & Horn, 2008, p. 65). These stressors also manifest themselves differently among new and mid-career faculty, women, parents and those responsible for eldercare, faculty of color, contingent faculty, etc. (e.g., Boice, 2000; Lindholm & Szelényi, 2008; Schuster & Finkelstein, 2006; Trower, 2012). And given the tendency for faculty members to set high self-standards, many of these stressors may be exacerbated by "unrealistic perceptions or by their limited ability to set and carry out goals" (Robison, 2013, xiii). Within these contexts, we define what productivity means to us within institutional contexts, and even a very brief review of the literature on stress and vitality has a great deal to say about the conditions under which faculty create these definitions.

## New Faculty

Supporting new faculty members in their transitions to both academia and specific institutional contexts has been the focus of extensive research in the past 30 years (see, for example, Austin, 2003; Boice, 1991, 2000; Sorcinelli, 2000). New tenure-track faculty tend to experience stress during the probationary period with respect to balancing time spent on research, service, teaching, and home life, especially when teaching their own classes for perhaps the first time. This stress can be exacerbated by having unclear expectations for promotion and tenure; building relationships in the department and institution-wide; and creating a professional identity in the traditional academic roles and as an advisor, colleague, institutional citizen, and community member (Austin, 2003; Boice, 1991; Eddy & Gaston-Gayles, 2008; Pojuan, Martin Crowley, & Trower, 2011; Sorcinelli, 2000).

## Mid-career Faculty

Mid-career faculty are the largest cohort in the academy and face unique challenges when moving out of the protected bubble junior faculty often function within (Baldwin & Chang, 2006, p. 28; Baldwin, Lunceford, & Vanderlinden, 2005, p. 98). Mid-career can be a double-edged sword in terms of stress and vitality (Baldwin, Lunceford, & Vanderlinden, 2005, p. 115). Researchers argue that, unlike new faculty who can aspire to promotion and tenure goals, mid-career faculty have achieved these goals and may enter a period when professional goals are in flux and less defined, which can lead to a loss of professional momentum (Baldwin et al., 2008; Canale, Herdlotz, & Wild, 2013). Yet mid-career faculty often have more opportunities to participate in research and take on greater leadership roles at their institutions (e.g., Baldwin et al., 2008; Canale, Herdlotz, & Wild, 2013; Stange, & Merdinger, 2014). Even with an array of new options for professional growth, mid-career faculty can enter a career plateau that affects their career motivation, engagement, and job satisfaction (Baldwin & Chang, 2006; Baldwin et al., 2008; Canale, Herdlotz, & Wild, 2013).

## Women Faculty

Women tend to experience more personal-professional tension when dealing with issues such as pregnancy, childcare, eldercare, and family leave politics, which can be compounded by department/institutional culture, a lack of role models, and individual perceptions of professional capital and expectations (Elliott, 2008; O'Meara, 2015; O'Meara & Campbell, 2011, p. 454). Women faculty report experiencing conflicting roles at work and at home, doing more housework and cooking at home, and juggling more of the childcare arrangements (Baldwin et al., 2008; Elliott, 2008, p. 159). This leads to high levels of stress related to time pressures, which one study showed to be significantly higher than male participants (Lindholm & Szelényi, 2008, p. 25). Women faculty also report a sense of "identity taxation," finding that their teaching loads and expectations for service and research productivity are higher than their male colleagues' (Baldwin et al., 2008; Eagan & Garvey, 2015; Elliott, 2008; Hart & Cress, 2008; Hirshfield & Joseph, 2012).

## Faculty of Color

A small percentage of the overall faculty in the US, many faculty of color report experiencing cultural taxation, which leads to higher service expectations than white faculty members, more student mentoring requests, and more demands to represent marginalized groups (e.g., Baldwin et al., 2008; Eagan & Garvey, 2015; Jayakumar et al., 2009; Padilla, 1994; Hirshfield & Joseph, 2012). Studies have found that faculty of color produce less scholarship than their white peers, perhaps due to increased service requests, increased effort needed to justify areas of scholarship considered "suspect" by senior peers, and subtle discrimination across all areas of work causing negative environments that affect productivity (Eagan & Garvey, 2015; Griffin, Bennett, & Harris, 2013). This subtle discrimination raises additional barriers to success in higher education for faculty of color, including a lack of mentors among peers, unsatisfactory relationships with senior faculty, higher but ill-defined standards for tenure and promotion, potential cultural misalignments, and general alienation and bias (Baldwin et al., 2008; Jayakumar et al., 2009; Pojuan, Martin Crowley, & Trower, 2011).

## Contingent Faculty

According to the American Association of University Professors (AAUP), non-tenure-track faculty (part-time, full-time, and graduate teaching assistants) accounted for approximately 76 percent of faculty, with more than 50 percent working part time (AAUP, n.d.). Issues surrounding contingent faculty are hotly discussed, especially issues of pay and benefits, resources, respect and support, job stability, preparedness, and effectiveness (see, for example, Cross & Goldenberg, 2009; Jaeger & Eagan, 2010; Kezar & Sam, 2011; Schuster & Finkelstein, 2006). Though many contingent faculty reported loving their teaching duties, they also cited terms of employment and issues of respect and inclusion as major sources of stress and dissatisfaction, specifically in terms of "low salaries, extended periods of work, excessive workloads, no physical space allocation on campus, and limited or nonexistent participation in departmental and institutional matters" (Levin & Montero Hernadez, 2014, pp. 543, 551; Whitman et al., 2012).

Given these cultural shifts and contextual stresses, O'Meara, Terosky, and Neumann (2009) identified an overwhelming "narrative of constraint" in reference to faculty lives, wherein words like "just making it," "treading water," "dodging bullets," and barely "staying alive" amid "scarcity, turbulence, and ambiguity" dominate discussions of the contexts in which we work (pp. 2, 3). Higher education scholar James Fairweather (2002) noted, "The ultimate tenet about faculty work, which is influenced by beliefs about the importance of intrinsic motivation and the overlap of teaching and research, is that faculty members can be productive in all aspects of faculty work" (p. 29). But Fairweather's study found that most faculty members cannot and do not achieve high levels of proactivity in all areas (p. 44). As faculty, we must make active choices about how to spend our time, based on personal and professional goals, commitments to institution and discipline, and necessary trade-offs, to create a fulfilling career and home life, which can be daunting, especially given the contextual challenges discussed above.

## Shifting the Narrative

The narrative of stress and constraint is only one side of a dynamic story about faculty life. O'Meara, Terosky, and Neumann (2009) also argue that a deeper, more motivating narrative with an "explicit focus on faculty growth" is equally at play (p. 2). They challenge faculty to "identify ways to foster . . . the desire and will to craft themselves as teachers, researchers, and partners in service and community engagement who have actively chosen, and continue to actively choose, the academic career as a way to lead their lives" (p. 19). A rich literature also explores how faculty can create careers that are meaningful, dynamic, and productive in the long term.

The research on vitality has shown that groups of faculty thrive in different environments with respect to O'Meara, Terosky, and Neumann's narrative of faculty growth. For example, new faculty report being most satisfied when tenure guidelines were clear and regular pre-review feedback was provided; policies and mentors supported different levels of work-life integration; and resources supporting all aspects of teaching and research were easily accessible. Furthermore, culture, climate, and collegiality, especially in terms of socialization and mentoring, were crucial in helping new faculty adjust to an academic career (Pojuan, Martin Crowley, & Trower, 2011; Trower, 2012). And mid-career faculty report satisfaction when they can focus time and energy on professional goals that motivate them most and develop "satisfying professional and social relationships with colleagues" (Huston, Norman, & Ambrose, 2007, p. 502; West, 2012). While speaking directly about mid-career faculty, Canale, Herdlotz, and Wild (2013) hit the nail on the head for all faculty when they note, "The challenge is for faculty to be responsible for their professional growth and development as an ongoing, career-long quest" (p. 6).

This work over the past 25 years supports Baldwin's (1990) findings that vital faculty have clearly articulated and concrete short-term and long-term goals that guide work in all aspects of their careers; these faculty can articulate specific projects they want to complete, take more professional risks, and actively look for growth opportunities, which leads to entrepreneurial and multidimensional careers over time (pp. 172, 174). This narrative of growth aligns closely with a 30-year tradition of research on faculty vitality, which is exemplified by Gooler (1991) as the faculty member "who is unremittingly curious, who feels a sincere commitment to both individual and institutional goals, who derives satisfaction from professional endeavors, who manifests behaviors that reflect enthusiasm for intellectual activity, and who looks forward to what the future may bring" (Gooler, 1991, p. 8, as cited in Kalivoda, Sorrell, & Simpson, 1994, p. 255). These vital faculty are "aware of their own career paths and . . . proactive in determining their goals and acting to achieve them" (Hardre, Cox, & Kollman, 2010, p. 10). Their definition of productivity is grounded in teaching and research but also in "intrinsically rewarding" and subtler forms of active engagement in the academy (Huston, Norman, & Ambrose, 2007, p. 518; Kalivoda, Sorrell, & Simpson, 1994, p. 260). Further describing vital faculty, DeFelippo and Giles (2015) argue that "challenge seeking, creativity, curiosity, energy, grit, growth mindset, motivation, optimism, and risk taking [as well as] productivity" are all characteristic of the vital faculty mindset. (p. 2).

In short, vital faculty are always searching for development opportunities to help them grow as professionals, and they can articulate specific projects that they find to be intrinsically motivating. Even stressful contextual challenges do not necessitate a narrative of constraint. This is a narrative of purpose, commitment, clearly articulated goals, growth, and vitality. And as we will see, this is a narrative of *Agility*.

## Introducing Agile and Scrum

Is it possible to integrate discussions about time, productivity, vitality, and goal setting in such a way that leads to a clear framework for faculty activities? Enter Agile and Scrum. Generally speaking, Agile is an increasingly popular work management ideology and set of productivity frameworks that supports continuous progress on work priorities even in the face of change. In its native software development environment, cross-functional Scrum teams, in coordination with a business liaison, set their own goals for work they will accomplish over a period of time, monitor their own progress, and actively and consistently reflect on their practices to ensure good products and engaged workers.

When I first learned about Agile, I was looking for new ways to encourage more authentic collaboration among my students during complex group projects. While I was trying to figure this out, my husband, a software engineer, moved to a web-based software company.

He began to talk about how they were using a new system, Scrum, to manage the application development process from management to design, development and testing, even marketing and technical writing. While Scrum took some getting used to, he found that the focus on encouraging teams to do their best work by trusting them, while building in accountability checkpoints, was helping to unite developers around common goals, a markedly different experience than he had had at other software companies.

Based on his recommendations, I started to do some reading and slowly implement aspects of the Scrum process into my course-based student projects. And as I taught my students these collaboration and project management strategies, I found myself applying them to everything from managing my own research agenda to course planning to trying to help the student organizations I advise develop more productive committee structures. Scrum, then, provided my students and me a framework for breaking projects down into discrete, actionable chunks, accomplishing these chunks within a self-designated time period, and visualizing progress toward goals.

Agile is an intentional shift away from the manufacturing mindset of project work to one that is more open to incremental but intentional progress and to a view of humans as the most valuable resource in an organization. For example, when you think about typical project management process for a research project, it might look something like figure 1.1. Figure 1.1 represents a linear, "waterfall" project management process common in manufacturing and other industries. In this process, extensive planning occurs up-front, and one step must be

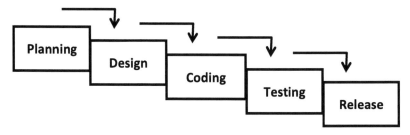

**Fig. 1.1** Traditional project management process

completed before the next can begin. For stable projects, waterfall can be an excellent approach. But in changeable environments or more ambiguous projects, waterfall can be a hindrance because it is relatively rigid—all the planning is done well before the project begins, setting up a process that can be hard to break out of if the context changes.

Agile and its most popular framework, Scrum, organize work differently, as shown in figure 1.2. Using Agile, I might begin a research project by brainstorming all the different activities that might potentially be necessary to complete the project, such as determining the goals of the project, collecting contextualizing literature, writing necessary preliminary documentation, testing and determining methods of data collection, collecting different types of data, etc. Next, I would group any smaller tasks under bigger chunks of work I must do, prioritizing activities that must be done before others (for example, piloting methods briefly before actually collecting data). I would then commit to completing a set of pieces within a certain timeframe (sprint), such as two weeks. I would work throughout the sprint on these specific tasks, perhaps checking in regularly with peers in my writing group

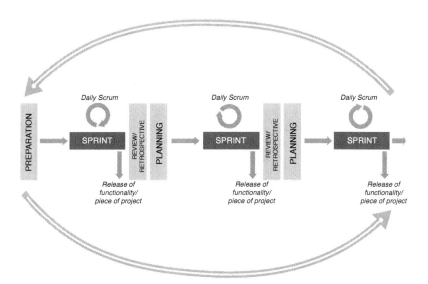

**Fig. 1.2** Scrum development process

for feedback. At the end of the sprint, I might share what I have completed with my writing group and then reflect on what went well, what I can do better, and what I want to do next. Finally, the process begins again when I update my project task list with any new tasks I might have thought of and choose new commitments for the next sprint. (See chapter 2 for a more detailed discussion of this process.)

Scrum is appealing to me personally because it provides an iterative framework and set of strategies for organizing my work that, when implemented successfully, can help me make and see progress on different projects. I can work on valuable pieces of the projects and have tangible outcomes at the end of a sprint. And because I am concentrating on smaller chunks rather than the entire project, I feel a greater sense of accomplishment throughout the process.

The Agile mindset and associated practices have grown increasingly popular not only in software development but also in graphic design and marketing, venture capital, journalism, and energy management, to name a few. A recent TED conference even included an "Agile parenting" talk (Feiler, 2013). The Agile practices and the values on which they are founded are not so different from our own as faculty, and the frameworks associated with Agile can help faculty focus on work that is most intrinsically meaningful; connect that work to the mission of the institution; and create personal satisfaction through "positive and passionate engagement" (Sutherland, 2014, pp. 147, 159). While certainly not a panacea that will solve all sources of faculty stress discussed above, Agile is another potentially productive means for faculty members to pursue the narrative of growth and vitality over the course of our careers.

## Origins of Agile and Scrum

Where exactly did Agile come from? Agile was a response to systemic problems in software development in the 1980s and 1990s, when consumers demanded more complex web-based applications than a traditional waterfall development process could support. A pioneering group of seventeen software developers met in 2001 at a retreat to discuss the overwhelming need to replace these management-driven, monolithic waterfall models, which they felt were harming the industry and its people through "Dilbert manifestations of make-work and arcane policies" (Highsmith, 2001). The result of that meeting was a philosophical foundation called the *Agile Manifesto*, which lists four specific guidelines, and a caveat, for valuing

> **Individuals and interactions** over processes and tools
> **Working software** over comprehensive documentation
> **Customer collaboration** over contract negotiation
> **Responding to change** over following a plan

> That is, while there is value in the items on the right, we value the items on the left more. (Beck et al., 2001)

The *Manifesto* addresses the perception common in many industries that the items on the right—processes, tools, documentation, contracts, and detailed plans—are necessary *before* a project can begin. Of course these are necessary, but Agile starts with the people and then adds process, encouraging transparency, collaboration, and adaptation in ways that traditional project management philosophies do not.

The *Manifesto* is important because the articulated value statements deconstruct the Taylorist approach that separated the people doing the work from the people planning the work, acknowledging that everyone in the software development process, from developers to customers, had something to offer the project and deserved respect (Fowler, 2005). The business analysts creating the product roadmap were just as important as the developers who coded it and the technical writers who wrote up the documentation—and they all had something to learn from one another to make the work better. By focusing on these underlying values, Agile encourages productivity through collaboration rather than production by loose cooperation. *Manifesto* signatory Martin Fowler (2005) claims that while a waterfall project might "go according to plan, a good Agile project will build something different and better than the original plan" (para. 49).

## Scrum Values

In addition to reflecting the foundational beliefs stated in the *Agile Manifesto*, Agile practices are grounded in a set of values that empower people to approach work toward meaningful goals with a growth mindset. Ken Schwaber, one of the original *Manifesto* signatories who helped to formalize Scrum with its chief architect Jeff Sutherland, added five additional values that allow teams to be mindful, as shown in table 1.1.

These values, though certainly challenging to align with consistently, encourage a very different way of thinking about work and productivity. The values encourage people and teams to focus on immediate goals and short-term wins rather than long-range objectives, to share knowledge rather than hoard it in silos, to take risks and own failures rather than assign blame elsewhere, and to respect the contributions and challenges of each person rather than keeping score. And while Scrum was designed to be enacted by teams, the *Manifesto* and Scrum values must be internalized by each member of the team individually in order to

TABLE 1.1  Descriptions of the Scrum values

| Scrum value | Description |
| --- | --- |
| Focus | Focus on and be accountable to the commitments the team has made without becoming distracted by other work or requests. |
| Commitment | Commit to the process and team-determined goals, and work realistically and honorably with every intention of completing the work. Commit to peers and to being the best professional version of yourself. |
| Openness | Create a truthful environment where people feel safe to voice dissent and concern, can accept help and constructive criticism, are transparent in their decision-making, and make all commitments and build all relationships in good faith. |
| Courage | Be willing and resolved to take risks that can benefit the project, to take ownership of and learn from failure. Support and defend the process. |
| Respect | Share progress, success, and failure with the team. Highly regard each person as offering something unique to the project, and assume everyone is doing their best at any given time. |

*Source:* Scrum Alliance, 2014.

be successful, therefore aligning the values with personal commitment as well.

The combination of the *Manifesto* with Schwaber's core values are the foundation for Scrum, which helps teams create better work that achieves more ambitious goals dependably over time. Agile coaching guru Lyssa Adkins (2010) perhaps sums it up best:

> Done most powerfully (and simply), Agile focuses us on the critical products to create and makes it possible for us to create them, one after another, most important after most important, in a way that allows us to meet our own high standards of excellence and pursue a vibrant personal purpose—but only when done well. (p. 5)

## Applying Agile to Faculty Work

To summarize some of the main points about Agile and Scrum from the previous section, Agile is about

having the courage to work toward big and meaningful goals knowing that the path may be windy with wins and setbacks along the way as you learn, grow, and help others in pursuit of those goals;

being flexible in the face of challenges and unexpected change, even welcoming it as an opportunity to review what you know and innovate to meet the challenge;

transparently sharing what commitments have been made toward achieving goals, achieving small wins regularly, and being open in sharing successes and setbacks in accomplishing that work so that everyone learns; and

creating an environment of respect based firmly on providing people with the support they deserve to accomplish meaningful goals and outstanding work, whether by active collaboration or servant leadership.

As faculty, we might not work under the same conditions as software developers, but our world is certainly based on sustained progress toward goals as well as personal and professional growth in all areas of our work. And as the academy continues to change, we can all use easy, actionable, and values-based strategies to manage these challenges, not just in the name of productivity or time management but also with the goal of continued, proactive professional progress and passionate engagement in the activities that led us to be academics in the first place. Here we truly begin to associate "Agile faculty" with a mindset of growth and vitality.

## An Agile Faculty Manifesto

Agile proponents outside of software development have offered up new interpretations of the *Manifesto* to spread Agile into different areas of work and life. My favorite version comes from blogger Dinah Saunders (2010), who reimagined the *Manifesto* for personal growth in five points:

> **Increasing individual flow using whatever works** over adherence to a system
> **Quality of life** over quantity of achievement
> **Small, quick decision making which works toward current goals** over detailed long-term planning
> **Simplicity** over complexity
> **Responding to change** over following a script

That is, while there is value in the items on the right, we value the items on the left more.

In this manifesto, Saunders narrows the original version that focused on direct collaboration activities to highlight individual quality of life, personalized trajectories, and small wins toward real goals. I appreciate this version because it reminds me of what is important in terms of personal and professional growth and the mindset I can adopt to achieve vitality in my career.

If we take our cues from both manifestos above, what might an Agile Faculty Manifesto look like? Remembering that Agile is a philosophical foundation for valuing work, I propose the following:

**Simplicity** over complexity whenever possible
**Quality of work-life accomplishments** over quantity of achievement
**Engaged learning** over passive reception
**Responding to changing environments** over maintaining status quo of academia
**Collaboration with students, colleagues, and communities** over isolated productivity

That is, while there is value in the items on the right, we value the items on the left more.

In proposing this faculty version of a manifesto, I hope to articulate that faculty work is both individual and collaborative. For individuals, this manifesto supports approaching personal work from the lens of simplicity and quality of work-life, recognizing that goals and environments will naturally change and that being open to that change is a necessary part of career vitality. The third point about engaged learning has a dual meaning; yes, it applies to pedagogy, but it also speaks to how faculty approach professional development and new challenges as growth opportunities rather than deviations from an existing path.

Collaboration is also a theme. It may not seem that faculty always work in the native collaborative environment of most Agile implementations, especially when working independently in the lab or poring over archival texts deep in the library. Yet we are all members of departments, schools, institutions, disciplines, and the broader community of higher education. We are always already working in collaboration with our students, research colleagues or disciplinary peers, committee members, and community partners. Higher education, somewhat like software development, is a collaborative venture that we each contribute to individually and as team players. And by enacting the first four values of the Agile Faculty Manifesto, we also serve as role models for peers and students in our attitude and approach to faculty work.

While the manifesto provides a philosophical grounding, additional values strengthen the ethical foundation.

## Agile Faculty Values

As discussed above, Ken Schwaber augmented the *Agile Manifesto* with five specific values that deepen the Agile mindset and approach. These five values further support the idea that Agile is philosophically different than traditional approaches to work and offer a foundation for thinking about productivity differently. What relevance do these Scrum values have to the Agile faculty perspective?

In 2007, Grappa, Austin, and Trice identified seven implicit values that drive faculty in the academy: equity, academic freedom, flexibility, professional growth, collegiality, autonomy, and respect. These values align nicely with Schwaber's five Scrum values, as shown in table 1.2.

**TABLE 1.2**  Alignment of Scrum and faculty values

| Agile value | Faculty value | Description |
|---|---|---|
| Focus | Flexibility | Allowance to personally prioritize work and life activities to make the most meaningful impacts (p. 141) |
| Commitment | Autonomy | Ability to make personal decisions about agendas to pursue and balance between faculty work and personal commitments (p. 141) |
| Openness | Academic Freedom | Protects privilege to "freely and responsibly express their views" in writing and in discussion "without institutional censorship" (pp. 140–41) |
| | Collegiality | Maintenance of a professional and developmental community of fellow scholars who support and value each other (p. 142) |
| Courage | Professional Growth | Regularly takes advantage of available opportunities to build capacities in research, teaching, service, administrative, and personal activities in pursuit of ongoing career vitality (p. 141) |
| Respect | Respect | Expectation of essential and "basic valuing of every faculty member" as a human being (p. 139) |
| | Equity | Expectation of fair treatment, access to resources, and faculty status regardless of appointment (p. 140) |

*Source:* Grappa, Austin & Trice, 2007.

Mapping faculty values to Scrum values reveals that, philosophically, faculty may already be somewhat aligned with an Agile mindset. The values of flexibility, autonomy, and academic freedom speak to personal and professional commitments, all of which must relate to the collective context of the larger institutional and disciplinary contexts. Scrum teams determine what slices of project work they will take on, and individual team members commit to contributing work toward those goals; though individuals may work independently, they check in with the rest of the team regularly to align their activities. Similarly, faculty appreciate collegiality, respect, and equity, which are inherently collaborative values. Being a good citizen of the academy requires some of the same commitments that Scrum team members make to their team, and both faculty and Scrum teams must support and model good citizenship for others.

Based on this philosophy and set of values, being Agile means being proactive, responsive, engaged, and resilient—all qualities many faculty aspire to engender in our students as well as ourselves. Keeping these values central when adapting Agile practices to accomplish meaningful faculty work can revitalize our professional activities in ways reflective of vital faculty.

### Enacting the Agile Faculty Mindset

Like successful Scrum teams working from the *Agile Manifesto* and values, vital faculty who are aligned with the proposed Agile Faculty Manifesto and values define success in terms of specific long-range personal and professional goals and, therefore, are more likely to achieve goals over time (Robison, 2012, p. 11). Agile faculty ask themselves "how committed do you feel to your goal?" rather than "how much progress do you feel you have made on your goal?" (McGonigal, 2012, p. 90). Agile faculty embrace Amabile and Kramer's (2011) progress principle, understanding that "of all the things that can boost emotions, motivation, and perceptions during a workday, the single most important is making progress in meaningful work (p. 4). And Agile faculty view their "entire career[s] as a work in progress . . . [and] are constantly trying to improve" and setting aspirational goals that are "high enough to be worthwhile achieving but low enough to be accomplishable" (Barber, 2013, para. 12, para. 8).

This is a book about one way to achieve this Agile faculty mindset through a set of practices from industry specifically adapted for faculty work. The chapters that follow offer practical advice and steps you can take immediately to adjust your approach to achieving your most meaningful goals in research, service, and teaching. The Agile faculty philosophy articulated in the manifesto and set of values above are implicit in each of the strategies discussed throughout. While adopting Agile cannot solve all the challenges that cause faculty stress, the strategies can provide a framework for making concrete and visible progress on the work you value most.

Chapter 2 lays out the specific terms, roles, and practices of the most common Agile framework, Scrum, as a place to start. I explain Scrum both in terms of the general practice of software teams as well as how I have implemented it in my own research, service, and teaching. This second chapter provides the foundation for the practical chapters that follow. The core chapters offer goal-driven strategies for

managing a personal research agenda (chapter 3);
coordinating collaborative research efforts (chapter 4);
leading productive committees (chapter 5);
mentoring students and peers (chapter 6);
planning a course (chapter 7); and
creating strong group projects and student teams (chapter 8).

These chapters are designed, for the most part, to be read independently, though I highly recommend reading chapter 2 before choosing a practical chapter to explore. Also, if you are most interested in the collaborative research approach discussed in chapter 4, I recommend reading chapter 3 on individual research agenda strategies first for a more well-rounded picture. While many of the chapters will touch on similar aspects of Scrum, each chapter offers something new or deeper than the previous ones. Choose whichever chapter seems to speak to a need in your work-life and see what strategies you can implement. The afterword is speculative—what would an Agile version of higher education look like? Is it possible? Might it be worth working toward?

I hope that you will find strategies to (re)align your faculty work with your biggest and most meaningful goals so that you are inspired anew to come to work every day and to inspire others along the way.

**2**

# Working the Agile Way Using Scrum

After reading this chapter, you will

- Understand the differences between traditional productivity management approaches and the Agile framework called Scrum
- See the ways that Scrum can be adapted to faculty work to organize time and resources more effectively when approaching important professional activities

If you think about your average day, if there is such a thing, you likely have a lot on your plate beyond traditional research, service, and teaching activities. Faculty are also subject matter experts, curriculum designers, educational technologists, advocates, advisors, mentors, assessors, and active members of our institutional, departmental, disciplinary, and local communities, just to name a few. This variety makes every day different and interesting, though it can sometimes be overwhelming to do everything well and in a timely manner.

In his book *Start with Why*, Simon Sinek asks some compelling questions:

What if we show up to work every day simply to be better than ourselves? What if the goal was to do better work this week than we did the week before . . . for no other reason than we want to leave the organization in a better state than we found it? (2009, p. 224)

Pushing all the stresses aside, these questions remind me why I chose an academic career: to leave my students and community better than I found them, every day, through my teaching and research and to be a better version of myself every day through those same activities. This mindset aligns well with the Agile mindset in that both can help us rethink "productivity" as the driving force in our work. Perhaps, like me, you sometimes feel that you are checking research, service, and teaching activities off a list to stay on top of "now" rather than actively engaging in these activities. I have found that Agile is one approach that helps me rethink daily activities as incremental but constructive steps toward the goals of bettering myself as a person and professional, collaborating with the people around me, and engaging my environment every day. I share this approach with you so that you might consider how Agile can help you achieve your goals as well.

This chapter introduces Scrum, an Agile framework for organizing professional projects around incremental but sustained progress toward goals. In this chapter, you will find a barebones outline of Scrum that gives you the foundation and terminology to explore how these strategies might play out in research, service, and teaching contexts, which are covered in the central chapters. The terms themselves are not as important as the concepts, but the vocabulary is a handy way to actively rethink what we tacitly do as we juggle many balls in the air at one time. Because Scrum focuses on supportive collaborations, clear understanding of what needs to be done at any given time, and positive professional values, it is an excellent match for faculty work, especially when we seek to pursue professional vitality, increase engagement, and think with a growth mindset.

Agile in software development is strictly team based, but the perspective of self-organizing teams can inform many faculty activities, both individual and collaborative. In the next section, I will walk quickly through a simplified version of the framework as it is used in software development, defining the cycles, roles, and necessary terms to understand the process. The goal here is not to start thinking about research or teaching as a "product" or as necessarily team based. Instead, the goal is to change the definition of productivity and to think about how to create value through Scrum's incremental and iterative approach. In the section after that, I will map the framework to faculty work by sharing examples from my own experience, so feel free to read whichever section appeals most to you.

## What Is Scrum?

Scrum[1] is an empirical Agile framework that provides a clear and collaborative set of processes to allow teams of professionals to plan, execute, and deliver excellent work consistently over time. The name "Scrum" is borrowed from a 1986 *Harvard Business Review* article (see Takeuchi and Nonaka) in which the authors compared highly productive cross-functional product development teams to a rugby move in which members of both teams lock arms and work to gain possession of the ball with their feet. If the team members don't collaborate well, they lose the ball (and people get hurt). Takeuchi and Nonaka argue that cross-functional collaborative teams allow for more innovation, more consistent productivity, and more flexibility in the face of changes over the development life cycle. They outline a process that several authors of the *Agile Manifesto* (see chapter 1), most notably Ken Schwaber and Jeff Sutherland, would formalize to what we now know as Scrum.

The goal of Scrum in its original software development environment is to regularly create functional working software that users can effectively implement to meet their needs. Most software these days is web based, as even Microsoft and Adobe have recently moved to cloud

---

1. My explanation of the Scrum process is based on nine years of reading, workshops, conferences, and personal experience. As such, I will cite only specific sources in this description when I use a direct quotation.

models to deliver large packages like Office and Creative Suite. Web application users will not wait for a year for new features or bug fixes. Everything successful Scrum teams do is based on short cycles of work in which the team commits to completing a piece of an application (incrementally) and to use the defined Scrum meetings at the beginning and end of a cycle to review what was created, adapt to any changes in what is needed, and plan for the next cycle. As Scrum creator Jeff Sutherland (2014) explains, "Scrum embraces uncertainty and creativity. It places a structure around the learning process, enabling teams to assess both what they've created and, just as important, how they created it" (p. 9).

## How Is Scrum Different?

Before Agile, most software development was done using a process directly borrowed from product manufacturing known as **waterfall** because each step of the process was completed before the next step could begin (see figure 2.1). As noted in chapter 1, the writers of the *Agile Manifesto* were reacting against waterfall's hierarchical structure in favor of people-driven development and adaptability to change.

Waterfall projects begin with extensive planning before the different stages of production begin and are characterized by the limited interactions people have with the group working on the previous or subsequent stage of the project. Waterfall is still the primary method of development in many large companies, but business analysts report that heavily plan-driven waterfall projects are often over budget and

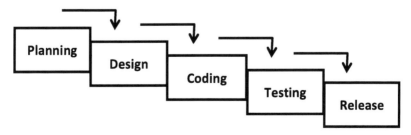

**Fig. 2.1** Traditional waterfall development process

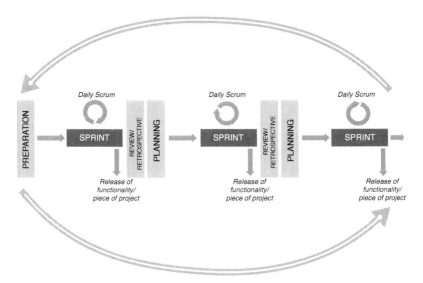

**Fig. 2.2** Scrum development process

late because there are no real opportunities to change course if needed once the detailed plan is set into motion. Sutherland (2014) argues that most waterfall projects in his 40 years of experience are built on extremely detailed plans that pretend to be able to see years into the future, which he says is akin to building your work on a fantasy rather than on reality (p. 119).

Scrum, on the other hand, provides a framework for working in and learning from much shorter cycles with full participation from team members, management, and stakeholders all committed to developing working products regularly (see figure 2.2). Rather than being plan driven like waterfall projects, Scrum projects are what we might call plan emergent. Time is taken at the beginning of new projects to outline the necessary features and goals for the product. Rather than defining every single aspect of the work up-front, teams commit to "opportunistic planning," which collaboration researcher Keith Sawyer (2007) explains as a process by which the working plan is understood to be a flexible outline that can be adapted as requirements and needs change during the work (p. 169). Through this process, wasteful activities can be reviewed, eliminated, and replaced by more effective strategies as people learn what works best for them and the project. Productive and satisfied faculty are quintessential opportunistic planners, and Scrum gives us a flexible framework to organize our activities without locking us into unnecessarily rigid plans whenever possible.

## What Is the Scrum Process?

When using Scrum in software development, a person from the business side (known as the **product owner** or **PO**) works with management and a cross-functional team of developers, architects, user experience designers, quality assurance testers, and sometimes technical writers and marketing professionals to maintain a prioritized list of pieces of software that must be built or revised to meet user needs. The list, known as the **backlog**, consists of **stories,** which are actions a user of the product should be able to take once the team completes each piece. Large, complex stories might be called **epics** by the teams, and the component work needed to complete the stories are called **tasks**. Epics and stories are most often written using a specific formula that helps the team understand the user and the motivations for each feature:

*As a <type of user>, I want to be able to <do something specific> so that I can <accomplish some goal or enjoy some sort of benefit>.*

Stories are considered ready for the team only when articulated as clearly and completely as possible. This may include **acceptance criteria**, which can be a combination of elements the final work must include to achieve the user's goals as well as all process steps the team must accomplish in order for the story to be considered complete, such as passing all quality assurance testing (also known as the "definition of done" for the team). The backlog of stories and acceptance criteria becomes the central working document from which the team pulls work to complete during the short work cycles.

At the beginning of a work cycle, usually a two- to four-week period called a **sprint**, the development team works with a team facilitator, the **Scrum Master**, to determine which of the highest priority stories realistically can be completed. These stories are moved into the **sprint** backlog, which the team then uses to collectively break stories down into component tasks, ask for clarification from the product owner about unclear points, estimate how much collective effort each will take, and discuss how they plan to complete the work in the sprint. This process is called **sprint planning**, and it's important to note here that while the product owner and the Scrum Master are involved in and facilitate the planning meeting, the team determines what stories to complete and then commits to that work; that teams self-organize is a mark of the Scrum values at play in this process. Teams commit to focusing on specific stories and tasks and openly share those commitments with the product owner, Scrum Master, other Scrum teams working on the application, and any relevant stakeholders, including customers.

Once the team members make sprint commitments, they visualize those commitments on a **Scrum board,** which is often a wall or large whiteboard. Each story is written on a large sticky note, and smaller sticky notes articulating each task that must be accomplished to complete the story are added as well. A basic Scrum board has three columns to track the progress of the work: Backlog, Work in Progress (WIP), and Done (see figure 2.3a below). Some teams add a fourth

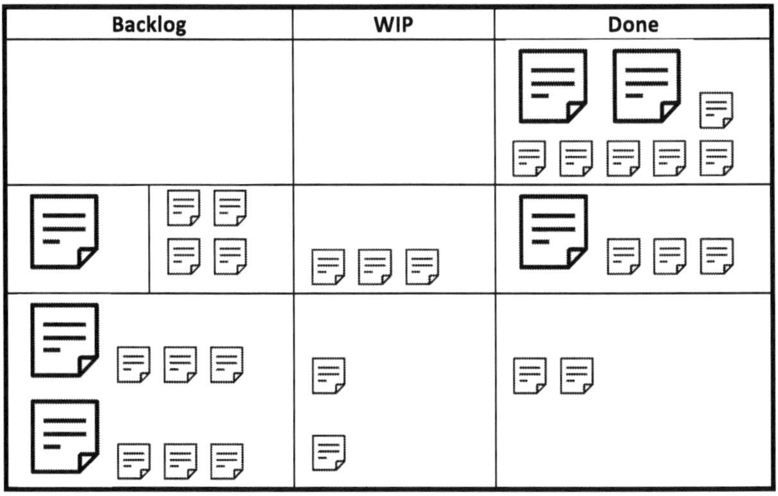

**Fig. 2.3a** Basic Scrum board

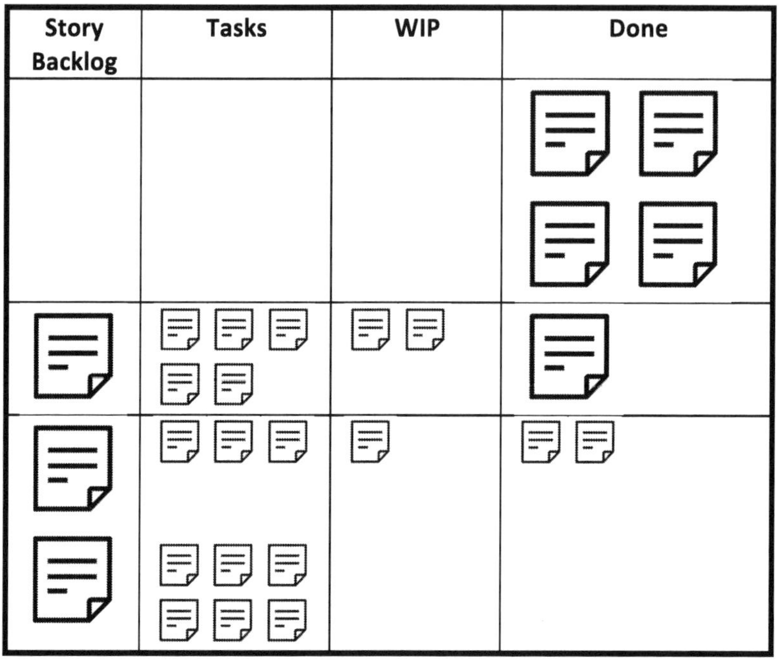

| Story Backlog | Tasks | WIP | Done |
|---|---|---|---|
| | | | 📄 📄 📄 📄 |
| 📄 | 📄 📄 📄 📄 📄 | 📄 📄 | 📄 |
| 📄 | 📄 📄 📄 | 📄 | 📄 📄 |
| 📄 | 📄 📄 📄 📄 📄 📄 | | |

**Fig. 2.3b** Modified Scrum board

column at the left of the board for large stories, placing the tasks in the second backlog column (see figure 2.3b).[2] The team then spends the sprint working to complete the stories. They physically move the sticky notes through the columns on the Scrum board, thus allowing everyone to see progress throughout the sprint, which reinforces transparency and productivity.

## What Happens during the Sprint?

To maintain high levels of accountability and collaboration, Scrum teams have several "ritual" meetings during the sprint. First, the team

2. Teams may use more columns, often called lanes, than the basic three, especially if they are using a combination of Scrum and another work management system such as Kanban or Kaizen. But each Scrum board requires only these three columns to be effective.

members and the Scrum Master meet every day, usually in the morn-ing, for a 15-minute meeting called **daily Scrum**, also known as a "stand-up" because the team stands in a circle to encourage a short meeting. Rather than a typical progress meeting, the daily Scrum is used to re-commit to team goals. Each team member answers three short questions:

> What have I done since we last met to meet our sprint goal?
> What will I do today to help us meet our sprint goal?
> What obstacles might impede progress that the team might be able to help me with? (Sutherland and Schwaber, 2013, p. 10)

This ritual serves an important purpose in addition to showcasing commitment and focus; it allows the team to regularly inspect both process and progress and to adapt on the fly if needed to meet their goals. It also encourages the Scrum values of respect and courage by normalizing the opportunity for team members to express challenges and ask for help, respecting that the team will respond to their requests helpfully rather than judgmentally. This approach, in turn, builds focus, courage, openness, commitment, and respect within the team. Other meetings might be called for members of the team to work on specific issues raised, but the daily Scrum is used only to discuss progress to-ward sprint commitments.

Once the pre-determined time limit for the sprint has elapsed, the team has two meetings as part of the commitment to openness. In the **sprint review**, members of the team do a demonstration of the work they completed during the sprint to interested parties. This might in-clude the product owner and management team, other developers, marketing and sales staff, other stakeholders in the organization, and even customers, who all provide direct feedback on the work. Feedback provides insight into what the team might need to keep working on in the next sprint, how this work fits with other pieces in development, and what changes might be addressed in the next sprint. Depending on the story and overall product plan, the work might then be pushed to production and released, or adapted into the backlog as new or revised stories.

Secondly, during the **sprint retrospective**, the team and the Scrum Master meet to reflect on their process during the sprint—what went well, what obstacles they faced, and what they can do better as a team. Keeping in mind the Scrum values of respect and courage, the Scrum Master facilitates the retrospective to focus on group improvement rather than potential finger-pointing if the process was not smooth. Based on this discussion, the team commits to improving no more than three aspects of the process during the next sprint. Thus, during every sprint the team is working on both product and process goals.

While the team members are working on sprint commitments, the product owner continues to serve as an intermediary between the business and development sides, **grooming** the backlog to make sure the stories are active and appropriately prioritized by adding and deleting stories when business goals, customer needs, or new information dictates.

Finally, the process starts again when the team meets with the product owner to review the groomed backlog and begins planning for the next sprint.

Using this approach, the teams take ownership for pieces of work they have committed to completing during the sprint. By visualizing their work, they not only showcase their commitments for everyone in the organization but also see their own progress as stories and tasks move across the board. Transparency, accountability, collaboration, and reflection are intentionally built into the system to help every person on the team accomplish his or her best work. In sharing work publicly, the teams might also help other teams solve shared problems or eliminate redundancies, unlike traditional work systems in which knowledge tends to be hoarded by individuals and teams. Using the Scrum framework, teams make incremental, regular progress toward larger goals, making deadlines more manageable and achievement more likely. This approach can translate successfully to faculty work in higher education, as discussed in the next section and the following chapters.

## How Have I Used Scrum in My Own Experience?

How might all of this translate to faculty members who probably (and rightly) do not think of faculty work as a "product in development"? It might be easy to make that leap when writing articles or manuscripts but probably not when engaging in teaching activities, mentoring, advising, and service. What appealed to me most about the Scrum process was the commitment to learning throughout the project due to the plan-sprint-reflect learning loop built in to it. As a preview of the chapters to come, here are three examples of how I recently used aspects of Scrum in my research, service, and teaching to illustrate how the Scrum process has affected the way I approach my faculty activities.

## A Research Example

Many research and writing projects can be and often are run in a waterfall manner. A waterfall writing process might look like figure 2.4. In this model, each stage of the writing process is completed before another stage is begun. This example might be extended to include a research agenda; some faculty may prefer to finish one project before moving on to the next to focus attention more narrowly. This linear process works quite well in many cases, though things can get more complicated when many projects are in progress, revise and resubmits are coming in with tight turnaround deadlines, and others join the project. Waterfall does not make it easy to adapt while maintaining steady progress.

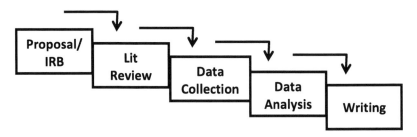

**Fig. 2.4** Writing an article using the waterfall process

I have been using the Scrum framework to coordinate my personal research agenda for several years now. Instead of keeping project to-do lists, I maintain my overarching project backlog in a Google Doc and use a physical Scrum board in my office to visualize different projects in progress. For example, a recent backlog contains three types of projects:

1. projects that are nearly complete, such as the revisions of accepted articles;
2. projects that are underway, including a pedagogy article about Agile in project-based learning that I am actively writing and a theory article connecting rhetoric and design thinking that I am researching; and
3. possible future projects, such as data collection on a spring curriculum pilot, data collection on a faculty work group I plan to lead next academic year, and the proposal for a student-oriented version of this book.

In my Google Doc, I treat each of these projects like an epic, which I then break down into component stories and tasks. When I am actively working on pieces of these projects, I transfer the appropriate stories and tasks to the physical board using markers and sticky notes. As I make progress on the projects of highest priority each week, I replace the completed task sticky notes with new notes for each new task I commit to for the upcoming week. My boards can be optimistic and messy—I like to leave as many sticky notes in the Done column as possible to remind me of my progress—but figure 2.5 shows a neat slice of my current board.

This process allows me to think carefully about what I can commit to and how to prioritize my research in relation to my teaching and service responsibilities that week. My goal is always to produce value during the week, whatever that might mean to me at the time. Perhaps more important is the psychological boost of seeing achievement on the Scrum board. I still use handy to-do lists for everyday work, but for larger goals, I have found Agile to be remarkably effective for me personally. Using a backlog, the sprint model, and a Scrum board, I am

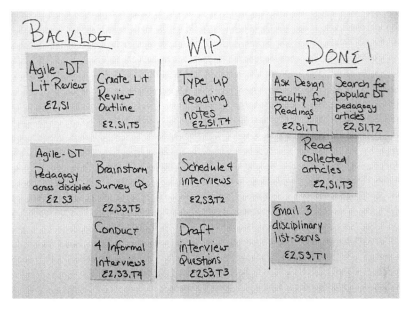

**Fig. 2.5** Research agenda visualized on a Scrum board

publishing more regularly, thinking more incrementally about my projects, and introducing different team strategies to co-inquirers.

Chapters 3 and 4 will explain in detail how you might adapt Scrum for your own individual and collaborative research projects.

## A Service Example

Recently, I introduced smaller aspects of the Scrum process to help committees in a large student organization be more productive. I advise an organization that has between 120 and 175 members at a given time and 11 committees responsible for philanthropy, scholarship support, public relations, and social engagement on campus. In the past, committee chairs did all the work and, as such, rarely achieved committee goals in more than minimal ways. I introduced a planning session at the beginning of each semester and a committee Scrum board—in this case a manila folder divided into three columns and smaller sticky notes—so that committees could better articulate what they wanted

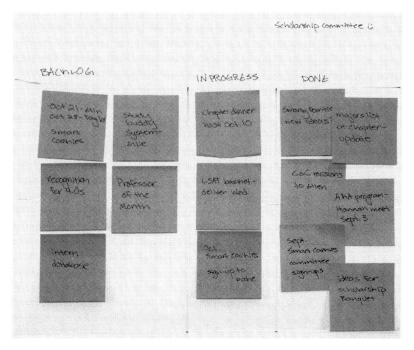

**Fig. 2.6** A student committee's Scrum folder

to accomplish during the semester and how they were going to do it. Figure 2.6 shows an example of a committee folder used by the organization's scholarship committee during the first semester we implemented the process and shows them thinking through both high-level goals and immediate tasks. Committees met every two weeks, and the folders were used to show progress and to provide information to the organization's leaders about how to better support the work of each committee.

Buy-in for Scrum in industry can be challenging because it is such a fundamental shift away from current work methods, and this group also showed resistance given the history of committees being only formalities. But the committee heads who committed to the process have seen greater involvement from their committee members and made more progress toward their articulated goals than other committees that chose not to use Scrum. Chapter 5 illustrates how you might implement Scrum to improve the work and engagement in committees and departments you lead. Chapter 6 covers how you might build on Scrum strategies when mentoring student advisees, undergraduate and graduate researchers, and faculty peers.

## A Teaching Example

I typically plan my project-based service-learning courses using the sprint model, teaching students how to use a backlog, stories and tasks, and the Scrum board to manage their teamwork as well as incorporating daily Scrum to encourage participation and accountability. After the students receive the basic project instructions, they brainstorm their project backlog based on the limited information they have, usually realizing early in the process that they will require stories for further research. They often realize that items they assumed were tasks were actually more complicated stories that needed to be broken down further. As they gain more information throughout the project by meeting with community partners, listening to other peer groups at end-of-sprint reviews, and simply working through their backlogs, teams add and subtract stories and tasks while grooming once a week, sometimes with me acting as their product owner.

Daily Scrums, for which I serve as Scrum Master, allow them to each report on their progress toward completing assigned tasks while holding each other accountable; it is difficult to hide in a project team when you know you will have to report what you have accomplished during every meeting. These meetings and their Scrum boards allow me to keep track of their progress, interject ideas and questions to help them be successful, and facilitate if group dynamics become an issue.

Table 2.1 shows the four sprints I recently used in a service-learning grant-writing class with a few of the associated stories. In the first two sprints, the students worked on foundational skills and a practice grant to prepare for the much longer sprint, during which they would be working with their community partners. Each sprint gave the students smaller goals to work toward, making the large grant in the third sprint

TABLE 2.1  Four sprints for a grant writing course

| Sprint | Associated preliminary stories |
| --- | --- |
| Professional development documents (1 week) | • Using rhetorical strategies<br>• Writing grants (overview)<br>• Identifying personal skills<br>• Writing strong resumes |
| Mini-grant (3 weeks) | • Understanding Calls for Proposals (CFPs)<br>• Developing the argument<br>• Conducting research<br>• Drafting the grant<br>• Revising against application criteria |
| Partner grant (9 weeks) | • Understanding Scrum<br>• Creating a team plan<br>• Working with a community partner<br>• Understanding the CFP<br>• Conducting research<br>• Developing the argument<br>• Revising with the partner<br>• Revising against application criteria |
| Funding decision (1 week) | • Creating a selection heuristic<br>• Evaluating applications<br>• Determining fair distribution<br>• Writing funding recommendations |

seem more manageable. Through reviews and team retrospectives at the end of each sprint, students could actively reflect on their grants and their writing processes, helping them plan opportunistically for the next stage of the project. Chapters 7 and 8 explore how Scrum can be used to design courses and student group projects.

I played different roles in each of these examples, from team member to Scrum Master and coach to product owner. Thinking about my role in each of these activities allowed me to step back and proactively control my actions rather than react to the unexpected, making me a better researcher, institutional community member, and instructor.

These examples provide a gateway to thinking about faculty work from an Agile perspective. The practical chapters that follow provide

specific, detailed, and actionable strategies you can implement immediately as an Agile faculty member.

## Wrapping Up

To summarize, Scrum offers a process framework that faculty can
adapt for different projects and styles of work. Scrum provides an empirical roadmap for how to approach any kind of faculty work without
constraining how that work is completed. The emphases on iterative
goal setting and incremental progress toward meaningful goals help to
make large projects less daunting and more actionable even as faculty
schedules are often anything but regular. The sprint model builds in
planning, execution, and reflection, a defined learning loop that faculty
often value in the classroom and as active, reflective, engaged academics. Scrum shifts the emphasis from *productivity* to active and engaging
*progress*, progress that might be slow but is also steady, transparent,
significant, and motivating.

The chapters are intended to provide jumping off points so faculty
can build the iterative, incremental learning loop into personal Scrum
implementations. Each chapter draws on specific aspects of the framework and roles to provide a broad picture of how Scrum might work in
an academic context. As noted earlier, this is not a waterfall text, so I do
not recommend reading the chapters in a linear order. I encourage you
to jump around and pick a chapter or section related to your current
interests. Only one caveat—chapter 4 on collaborative research builds
on strategies discussed in detail in chapter 3 on individual research. If
you are most interested in collaborative research, I highly recommend
reading both chapters. Otherwise, read, plan, execute, reflect, adapt,
and then try a new chapter. Happy sprinting.

# 3

# Organizing and Prioritizing Your Personal Research Agenda

After reading this chapter, you will be able to

- Convert a research project to-do list into an easy-to-manage project backlog with epics, stories, and tasks
- Plan effective sprints using the prioritized research backlog to make consistent progress toward meaningful goals
- Visualize your active sprint backlog using a Scrum board to track research progress

Faculty life is a balancing act, and elements of the research, service, and teaching triangle rarely seem equilateral. Faculty at different types of institutions must address institutional priorities while pursuing professional goals that sometimes align but, at other times, do not. Add family life, personal interests and hobbies, and time for simple reflection, and the calendar becomes more complex.

Agile and Scrum translate well to different contexts because they provide an active framework to manage complexity. Once I started using Scrum to organize student collaborative projects, I also realized how it could help me organize my own faculty work. My university is a teaching-focused institution with a tradition of excellent teaching and extensive service in addition to a growing emphasis on research. In my first years on the tenure track, I struggled to find time for research and writing during the regular semesters. Eventually, I found that implementing a Scrum approach helped me to balance teaching and service while focusing on the research activities that would produce the most value toward my meaningful goals at the time.

This chapter introduces three Scrum strategies that can be used to create stability in research and writing activities with focus, commitment, and openness. I explain how to replace the high-level to-do list with a research agenda backlog, use stories and tasks to create actionable chunks of work, and create a visual board to track progress. By openly visualizing commitments to both big picture and immediate progress, faculty can focus on honoring personal commitments rather than just "being productive."

## To-Do List vs. Backlog

Why are lists so popular, and why are so many well-liked productivity management systems today built on the humble list? People like neat, spatial ordering of information into digestible chunks. Lists in general allow us to outline main points clearly for readers and make it easy for us to skim what we read for important information. Bloggers and online media writers have exploited this preference for years, the pop culture website *Buzzfeed* being the most egregious example. As I type today, a brief scan of websites I regularly visit revealed these headlines: "5 Things to Start Your Day" (*CNN*), "5 Work Stresses You Can Alleviate with Tech" (*Harvard Business Review*), "How to Make Privacy Policies Better, in Two Easy Steps" (*The Atlantic*), "What 11 Successful People Wish They'd Known about Money in their 20s" (*Business Insider*), and "3 Problems with a Bias for Action" (*Inside Higher Ed*). Personal to-do lists help us keep track of small tasks we want to accomplish in a day or week, but problems can arise when we create tasks that are too large or complex, don't prioritize tasks on the list, or add new items without completing old ones (Jones, 2014; Marriott, 2015).

Researchers studying productivity and procrastination have long argued that unfulfilled tasks can harm our progress toward goals by pulling our focus away from what we can do immediately and to the overwhelming whole of what we need to do eventually. Bluma Zeigarnik, a Soviet psychologist and psychiatrist during the Gestalt movement, identified what is now known as the Zeigarnik Effect, showing that people remember unfinished tasks more than finished tasks and that those unfinished tasks weigh heavily on our minds (Baumeister & Tierney, 2011, pp. 80–84). Masicampo and Baumeister (2011) also found that study participants who were interrupted when doing an initial task did worse on later tasks, while those who were asked to make a plan to finish the first task did much better on the following tasks because they were not dwelling on the unfinished activity.

Agile strategies are built, intentionally or not, on the core ideas of the Zeigarnik Effect and the psychological value of openly focusing on specific and timely commitments. Even if a to-do list works perfectly well for you for keeping track of everyday tasks, as it does for me, a complete research agenda backlog can allow you to reimagine larger projects and their components to produce the psychological boost of creating a plan that is flexible, adaptable, and always accessible.

As discussed in chapter 2, a backlog is built on the hierarchy of epics, stories, and tasks. Epics can be written to articulate the purpose, object, and goals of a project, while stories can be written to highlight the purpose, object, and goals of a smaller aspect of a project. Tasks are the micro-level in this scheme, the tactical steps one must complete to finish the story and eventually the epic. Table 3.1 illustrates the major differences between a research agenda articulated as a to-do list and as an Agile backlog. When I used a general list, it served as a reminder of the projects in various stages of development that I was working on at the time; I wrote the project titles out on sticky notes that I posted on the wall in my office near my computer screen. While this reminded me of my active projects, the list did not remind me why each project

**TABLE 3.1** Comparison of my research agenda as list and as a backlog

| To-do list version of research agenda | Backlog version of research agenda |
| --- | --- |
| • Design thinking literature review<br>• *Metis* and design thinking theory article<br>• PWR/Comm course service learning partnerships project<br>• *Agile Faculty* manuscript revisions<br>• Agile and design thinking in PWR research methods service learning course<br>• Metic and design thinking in TPC survey study | Epic 1—As the only researcher applying Agile and Scrum practices to faculty development, I want to publish a faculty development text that clearly translates the Agile mindset and Scrum practices so that faculty can successfully implement these strategies in all aspects of their work to improve progress, balance, and career vitality.<br><br>Story 1—As a faculty member who has used Scrum practices to manage my research, I want to revise chapter 3 so that readers can immediately implement the strategies I outline in their research.<br><br>Story 2 (chapter 4), Story 3 (chapter 9), etc.<br><br>Epic 2—As a researcher interested in the intersections of rhetoric, *metis*, Agile, and design thinking, I want to better understand the relationship between these concepts in practice so that I can develop innovative pedagogical approaches and new knowledge to share with peers in the discipline.<br><br>Story 1—As a researcher just realizing the intersections between Agile and design thinking, I want to conduct a systematic literature review about design thinking so that I can clarify my own thinking about the connections.<br><br>Story 2—As a researcher exploring the intersections between *metis*, Agile, and design thinking, I want to build on my previous *metis*/Agile article by adding theoretical research about design thinking to continue building this line of argument in the field.<br><br>Story 3—As a researcher exploring the intersections between *metis*, Agile, and design thinking, I want to better understand how other instructors in the discipline might be knowingly or unintentionally teaching metic and design thinking strategies so that I can paint a picture of existing applications in the discipline and innovate in my own work. |

was important to me, how complete the project was, or what I could do next to make a productive step forward.

The right column of table 3.1 shows a portion of my active agenda articulated as epics and stories. The story formula forces me to convey a deeper rationale for each project and to break the projects down into smaller chunks of work that can be tackled individually. The first epic in the backlog, for example, reminds me (1) that my work is unique, (2) that I have a planned pathway to share that work with an audience who might respond well to it, and (3) that the work serves to help a population of people about whom I care deeply: fellow faculty. Compare that to the list version of the same project, "*Agile Faculty* manuscript revisions." Not nearly as inspiring or encouraging, is it? Framing a research agenda in epics and stories can be both inspirational and aspirational while also creating a pathway to completing the work you value. The next section of this chapter—perhaps ironically—provides a list of steps faculty can take to convert a research agenda into a research backlog.

## Create Your Research Agenda Backlog

According to Mike Cohn (n.d.), a leading Agile author and consultant, the product backlog in a software project is a "prioritized features list, containing short descriptions of all functionality desired in the product" (para. 1). He notes that the backlog is "allowed to grow and change as more is learned" (Cohn, n.d.). Perhaps the most important words in Cohn's description of the backlog are "prioritized" and "grow and change"; the backlog, like a faculty research agenda, is neither static nor inflexible nor haphazard. Using a research agenda backlog can help you to articulate, prioritize, and commit to doing valuable pieces of research. Essentially, faculty can begin to actively function as personal product owners.

The initial act of creating your research agenda backlog can feel a little intimidating because the goal is to get everything you are working on or plan to work on in the near future down in one document. If you are like me, this might be something you do already. Perhaps you keep an open document to which you add project ideas as they occur to you, or maybe you create master plans for each semester and summer.

Because creating a research agenda backlog is a one-time process, it can be an opportunity to see the fascinating projects you are working on or want to work on in the future all prioritized in one place. I recommend setting aside a specific amount of time for brainstorming the complete backlog, about an hour, so that you don't begin to feel overwhelmed by the amount of work you "need" to do. Realize you aren't likely to complete everything in the backlog because the list will change and evolve as you do; be comfortable with that knowledge (Sutherland, 2014, p. 174). The backlog should be exciting and full of possibilities rather than daunting.

To create a research agenda backlog, follow these steps:

1. **Open one new document, and save it somewhere easily accessible.** While it might seem more logical and manageable to create one document for each project, part of the Agile system is to be able to see everything in one place and be able to access the list whenever you need it. Like "the software application" is the subject of a Scrum team's backlog, your "research agenda" is the subject of this backlog. I have a backlog Word document saved in my Dropbox folder (www.dropbox.com) so that I can access it from whatever computer I happen to be working on. Choose your preferred medium—Word document, Google Doc, spreadsheet.

2. **List all research-related projects, active and near future.** The backlog contains all the work you will do or hope to do, so allow yourself to add not only your active projects but also the ones you might do as the research agenda progresses. Give each project a title, and put it in the backlog file as a heading or epic. If not fully formed enough to have a title yet, add it to a separate space at the bottom of the backlog until you are ready to shape it further.

3. **Turn the projects into epics and stories using the appropriate format.** Whether you begin with epics or stories will depend on how your list is structured. If the list contains high-level project statements such as my sample list in table 3.1, begin with epics and then move on to stories for each. If you have listed smaller

chunks of bigger projects, create the stories, group them under specific projects, and write an overarching epic to pull those stories together. Try using this modified story format:

> As a <type of researcher/instructor/faculty member>, I want to <create something> so that <I or my audience can know/ do/achieve something>.

4. **"Brain-dump" every task you might need to complete to make progress on each story** (see table 3.2). This is the part that most closely resembles creating a to-do list. A story in a research backlog is a portion of work that must be accomplished to complete the project, but that story breaks down into smaller tasks. What activities must be completed to call each epic and story "done"? List everything you can think of for each project on the agenda; remember that the research agenda backlog is not a to-do list for the week, or even the semester, but an aspirational document. Your backlog is your master plan to help you take advantage of the Zeigarnik Effect—all your "unfinished tasks" are in a list you can access whenever you are ready to plan.

**TABLE 3.2**  Excerpt from my Agile research agenda

| Epic 2 | Story 1 | Story 1, Task 1 |
|---|---|---|
| As a researcher interested in the intersections of rhetoric, *metis*, Agile, and design thinking, I want to better understand the relationship between these concepts in practice so that I can develop innovative pedagogical approaches and new knowledge to share with peers in the discipline. | As a researcher just realizing the intersections between Agile and design thinking, I want to conduct a systematic literature review about design thinking so that I can clarify my own thinking about the connections. . . . | Informally interview colleagues in art and graphic design to generate list of top design thinking texts. |
| | | Story 1, Task 2 |
| | | Conduct academic journal database search to locate most popular texts about design thinking. |
| | | Story 1, Task 3 |
| | | Conduct database search for publications that discuss both Agile and design thinking. |

5. **Prioritize your backlog.** The final step in creating your research agenda backlog is to prioritize both the projects and the stories within the projects. Start with the projects, and order them according to priority, i.e., whichever tasks have the most potential to produce value immediately (Sutherland, 2014, p. 121). Which is closest to being done? Which is most important for you to complete or advance? What are you the most excited about? Once you've ordered the list according to your priorities, similarly order the stories and tasks within each project. Prioritize anything that can be accomplished quickly or that must be accomplished before other stories can be activated.

While the process of creating the research agenda backlog might seem a little intimidating at first, it need be done only once if done well. You can then simply maintain the backlog by adding or deleting epics and stories and reprioritizing as necessary over time. In this way, you are acting as a product owner for your research agenda, continually assessing, keeping track of, and reprioritizing the pieces of your work that will produce the most value over time. That value can be progress toward an article or book, setting up a new and exciting project, or allowing time to think through new pathways. The backlog is a living document that can be adapted easily by adding or subtracting items in response to change and personal interests. The backlog can also be a reality check that illustrates how priorities may be actively competing with one another. Done well, the backlog can show where your true interests and commitments are.

Rather than working day-to-day from the entire backlog, you can now use it as the research agenda hub, the place to go to pull out projects and activities to work on intentionally for a specific amount of time. Because all possible projects and tasks are written down, you do not have to use extra brainpower to keep track of them. As researchers Masicampo and Baumeister (2011) found, humans work better with a flexible plan that allows for interruptions, a reality of faculty life. Maintaining a flexible backlog can encourage focus on what's important to your goals at any given time.

### New Faculty and Department Chairs

As a department chair, working through this process early in a new faculty member's career, perhaps together, provides an excellent opportunity to talk about managing competing priorities, working toward promotion and tenure requirements, and defining the role of research progress for faculty in the department.

## Build a Realistic Sprint Plan from the Backlog

Being productive with Agile strategies is all about knowing what you might do and what you can realistically *commit* to in a set amount of time (Sutherland, 2014, p. 175). In non-Agile software environments, development teams often work toward quarterly goals. They know what they have to do, but typically most of the work will get pushed off until the last minute, causing developers to work overtime and late into the night to meet team goals. These developers are not lazy or unprofessional. They are often just responding humanly to deadlines that seem far off. How often have you said, "Oh, I have three months to do that peer review; I'll get to it next week"? Three months later, you're scrambling to get it done on time, or at least I am, cursing yourself for putting it off so long.

To mitigate these natural tendencies, the Scrum framework breaks goals into smaller, more manageable sprints (see chapter 2). During your sprints, you commit to completing specific stories from your backlog in order to move your research agenda forward. In software development, sprints are usually anywhere from two to four weeks. To plan your first sprint from the research agenda backlog,

1. **Commit to a sprint timeframe**. I typically create a semester backlog from my larger plan then divide that up into two-week sprints, which I have found works best for me. Play with the different time frames, and see what works best for you. To get

started, I recommend a two-week sprint because it allows you to test out how accurate your estimates are in terms of what you can accomplish in a given time frame. If you set a long sprint at first, you might fall into the trap of waiting until the last minute to complete sprint commitments.

2. **Pull priority stories and tasks from the research agenda backlog into the sprint backlog.** If you organized your research agenda backlog well, pull the stories from your top priority projects into a temporary document. Think about what you can accomplish during the sprint and how to most effectively mix tasks. Are you really close to finishing a revise and resubmit? Pull only the stories associated with that project into the sprint backlog. Can you collect survey data at the same time without spreading yourself too thin? If yes, pull some of those initial data collection tasks into the sprint backlog as well. Rather than asking yourself, "What can I accomplish this sprint?," try asking, "What will I *commit* to accomplishing this sprint?" That little shift in perspective can have surprising impacts on motivation to accomplish goals.

3. **Remove a few things from your sprint backlog.** Let's be realistic—unless you are on sabbatical, you probably have teaching and service responsibilities during your sprint as well. Those are important priorities that will take up time, and rightly so. To start with, set some small but doable goals for the first few sprints until you find a rhythm that works best. Once you've gotten a sense of what, in Agile terms, is called your "velocity," set future sprint commitments accordingly. But until then, strike a few things off the first sprint backlog. Remember, the sprint backlog is a *commitment* to focus on projects that are important right now. Focus on small chunks of work and incremental progress; the research agenda backlog will be waiting for you when the time comes to choose new commitments.

At this point, you might be thinking that you have created a different set of to-do lists, so what makes this process different or Agile? One of the key ways Scrum holds people more accountable to commitments is through visualizing the work activities.

## Make Your Sprint Backlog Visible

While the backlog allows you to see the bigger picture of your research agenda and projects, visualizing the work on a Scrum board allows you, and others, to see it in a different way. Scrum teams use boards or walls to visualize the flow of work at every stage of progress. Depending on what Agile methodology the team is using, they might refer to it as the Scrum board or Kanban (Japanese for "card" or "sign board"), but fundamentally the features and benefits are the same. All you need to get started is an empty wall, the back of a door, or a white board; a set of multi-colored sticky notes appropriately sized to your board; some dark pens or markers; and your sprint plan.

To visualize your sprint,

1.  **Divide your board or space into three columns, and label them, in order from left to right, "Backlog," "Work in Progress" or "WIP," and "Done."** How you physically divide your board obviously depends on where your board is and what it's made of. You might use a ruler and a dark dry erase marker to create your columns on a whiteboard. If you have the benefit of a large wall or door, you might use painter's tape to mark off the columns. Or you might tack up large pieces of drawing paper to cover the back of a door and draw your columns with a marker.
2.  **Transfer items from your sprint backlog onto individual sticky notes.** Write each story and task onto a separate sticky note, and arrange the notes on the board in the Backlog column. I like to use a different color to represent each project and give each project its own row. You might assign different colors to different priority tasks, instead; do whatever makes the most sense to you.
3.  **Prioritize the sticky notes in the Backlog column on the board from most to least important.** If you move your stories and tasks directly from backlog to board, you probably already

have the projects in priority order from top to bottom. But take a minute to make sure you are comfortable with the order of the projects on the board and with your commitment to the work for the sprint. For example, I might put my data collection project at the bottom of my board for this sprint because it's an ongoing project, but the almost finished article I'm trying to get out for review tops my board as my main focus.

Figure 3.1 shows an example of what a generic sprint backlog for a one-month sprint might look like, with the longer boxes representing stories and the smaller ones representing tasks.

Figure 3.2 and table 3.3 show two versions of a one-month summer sprint based on my sample research agenda above. I prefer to use a physical Scrum board rather than software because the act of examining the board and physically moving tasks across the board helps me feel productive (see figure 3.2). Software could work just as well, though. Complete epic and story statements are lengthy given the level of detail and, therefore, difficult to write out completely on a standard sticky note. Table 3.3, then, illustrates a paper-based version of the sprint that I might keep as a Word document on my desktop for the

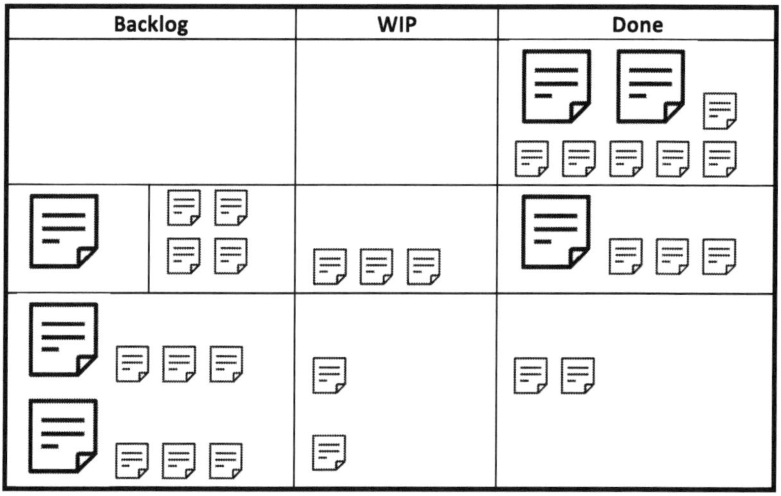

**Fig. 3.1** Sample Scrum board

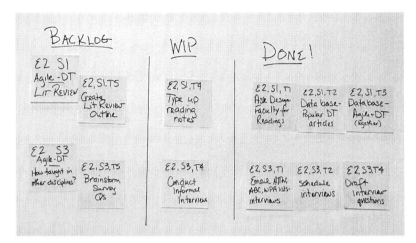

**Fig. 3.2** Physical Scrum board of a sprint in progress

**TABLE 3.3** Paper-based version of sprint in progress

| Sprint backlog | Work in progress | Done! |
|---|---|---|
| Epic 2, Story 1—As a researcher just realizing the intersections between Agile and design thinking, I want to conduct a systematic literature review about design thinking so that I can clarify my own thinking about the connections. | Task 3—Conduct database search for publications that discuss both Agile and design thinking. | Task 1—Informally interview colleagues in art and graphic design to generate list of top design thinking texts.<br><br>Task 2—Conduct academic journal database search to locate most popular texts about design thinking. |
| Epic 2, Story 3—As a researcher exploring the intersections between *metis*, Agile, and design thinking, I want to better understand how other instructors in the discipline might be knowingly or unintentionally teaching metic and design thinking strategies so that I can paint a picture of existing applications in the discipline and innovate in my own work.<br><br>Task 5—Brainstorm possible survey questions based on interview responses. | Task 4—Conduct informal interviews (already IRB approved). | Task 1—Email ATTW, ABC, and WPA listservs asking anyone using design thinking or Agile in their professional communication courses to contact me for a quick interview.<br><br>Task 2—Schedule interviews for each respondent.<br><br>Task 3—Develop short list of questions about design thinking, Agile, and *metis* for interviews. |

sprint duration. It contains the full statements so that I can reference them before updating the physical board. To ensure the epics, stories, and tasks fit onto the physical board, I then transfer shortened versions to sticky notes, which I arrange appropriately.

Once you transfer the sprint backlog to the board, as I did in figure 3.2, it becomes the hub for the sprint, the place where you select a task to work on and openly show progress as you complete tasks. Using the board on a regular basis is a way to recommit to goals and choose a task to focus on whenever you have time. To use the board effectively,

1. **Start the sprint by moving the one or two top priority tasks or stories into the WIP column.** These represent the tasks that you commit to completing first or quickly. Limiting the number of tasks in the WIP column is important. Pick a few tasks, and focus on those activities.

2. **As the sprint continues, work on a WIP task first, then move the sticky note representing that task into the Done column when you are finished.** Focusing on the WIP tasks helps narrow your work into manageable chunks. As you start to move tasks into the Done column, you can see your progress, as can anyone else who sees the board. I hang my board in my office just to the right of my desk so that I can see it regularly, as can anyone who visits.

3. **Once a task is moved to Done, select another task from the Backlog column, and move it to the WIP column.** If you've prioritized the sprint backlog well, this should be a seamless rather than agonizing choice. Trust your plan, and move to the next task.

Continue this process throughout the sprint until you have completed all tasks by the sprint end date. For example, before leaving each day, I update my board, moving any completed tasks into the Done column and patting myself on the back for meeting my commitment to myself. I often reflect for a few moments to reconfirm that I am happy with the tasks in the WIP column, perhaps adding one task or story to replace a Done item or making a mental note to work on a specific task or two the next day.

In this way, I act as my own Scrum Master in addition to product owner (and team); I reflect on my process and articulate my learning as I work through my research activities, while also acknowledging when I might be stuck and need help. Visualizing work on the Scrum board makes it easier to bring a colleague into the process when I do need assistance or to talk about a problem. This allows me to be honest with myself about progress toward my commitments and to remember why I committed to them in the first place.

### Department Chairs

Visualizing a research agenda in your office and showing slow but steady progress toward your own goals can serve as a model and a discussion starter for your faculty.

## Remain Agile in the Face of Change or Opportunity

Hopefully, by the end of a sprint, you have met your sprint goals. But we all know how things can crop up—student conferences take longer than expected, the chair needs you to complete a report quickly, your child gets the flu, or a surprising trend in preliminary data shifts the entire project. Don't be frustrated. Be Agile.

One of the core tenets of Agile is to be flexible and adaptable in the face of change, rather than resistant. Change is simply a part of our work lives, not something we can or should avoid or ignore. Because the research agenda backlog is a living document and you are your own product owner, you can always add or remove items from the list without sullying a neatly organized, in-pen to-do list. Think of the backlog as the work you want to do but not the active plan to do it; that plan comes in your sprinting. Priorities in the backlog are always in flux, and embracing that uncertainty makes for a more gratifying journey (Sutherland, 2014, p. 189). It's your research agenda to adjust as your interests grow and your priorities (or available time) change.

Updating a sprint plan is as easy as removing a few sticky notes and replacing them with others. Sticky notes are cheap and as flexible as you need them to be. While a Scrum purist would argue that you should not change commitments during a sprint, you decide what is an interruption and what is an opportunity. An unexpected data collection opportunity might be important or unique enough to shift priorities mid-sprint. But a promising pattern in preliminary data might wait until the end of the sprint; add it to the research agenda backlog, and continue with your sprint commitments. I do not recommend changing the sprint backlog midstream, which often interrupts the commitments you have made to immediate goals. But being Agile means being responsive to opportunity and using the system to respect your research even as priorities change.

## Wrapping Up

In this chapter, you learned how to create a research agenda backlog, to divide that work into productive sprints, and to visualize your work. The one-time investment of creating a research agenda backlog can change the way you commit to and honor your research or writing. Articulating and visualizing research projects using a Scrum board is an easy way to regularly see these commitments and progress. This method requires some up-front work to get started and minimal time later, time that you can use to work on your projects and reflect on your successes.

In the next chapter, I will look at how Scrum functions for collaborative research teams, which is closer to the native environment in which Agile processes were developed. Chapter 4 extends the strategies discussed here, focusing on how to scale the Scrum process in different team environments and using it to coordinate the work of multiple people.

# 4

# Running a Collaborative Research
# Project or Program

After reading this chapter, you will be able to

- Lay the groundwork for effective research collaborations
- Build a project backlog with the team and implement strategies for estimating and prioritizing stories to effectively organize the backlog
- Adapt two Scrum structures depending on the project: a strategy for organizing one team working on one large project and a strategy for coordinating smaller projects being completed under the banner of one agenda

Faculty research is always collaborative, as we take part in the conversations of our disciplines through conferences, publications, casual debate, and workshops; research is not done in a vacuum, and faculty contribute knowledge to the disciplines in the hope of making an impact. Interdisciplinary research and Scholarship of Teaching and Learning (SoTL) in the United States, as well as a general move toward cooperative work, are increasingly valued in higher education. Consider two hypothetical situations:

Four former classmates from a master's in nursing program are all now clinical faculty at different schools across the country. They meet for lunch at a professional conference, discussing teaching methods they use for a tricky area of the undergraduate curriculum. They all face the same pedagogical challenge, and they each have approached it differently. One nurse suggests a collaborative research project to study this challenge using a SoTL approach, to which they all agree. Before the end of the conference, they work out several joint research questions and a plan to study a problem-based learning intervention in their introductory courses.

A post-graduate in biochemistry arriving for his first day at a new research lab in a large R1 institution is greeted by the lab manager and invited to the lab meeting in 15 minutes. At the meeting, the broad scope of the work being done becomes more clear. Under the theme of genetic sequencing to improve cancer treatments, he counts 10 active projects in the lab with at least 25 people working on them. Some of the projects are closely aligned and seem to depend on the results of others, while half seem more independent. The head of the lab, a famous medical researcher, listens to the verbal reports, grills the researchers on the status of projects and articles, and offers advice for problems. After the meeting, the biochemist moves to his assigned lab bench and reads up on the project he'll be joining.

Creativity research (see Amabile, 1996, 2011; Csikszentmihalyi, 2008; Nussbaum, 2013; Sawyer, 2008, 2012) shows over and over again that more heads are better than one, to a point, and that innovations depend at least on wide-ranging thinking, reading, and talking to spawn connections between seemingly disparate ideas. The faculty in the hypothetical situations above have created or joined projects that will draw on the efforts of each team member to create results that are generalizable beyond one intervention or experiment. But collaboration is difficult in any situation, perhaps even more so in academic research when the researchers are all highly educated, independent thinkers who may not have training in managing large, complex projects. Add the potential complication of research team members being distributed across different universities and countries, like the nurses in the first example, compounded by limited time or varying priorities, and the probability of problems and frustration skyrockets. Agile and Scrum are based on similar complex collaborative situations in software development, and these strategies can be directly translated to successfully manage collaborative academic research to help overcome these challenges.

In this chapter, I will first review some research on the collaborative mindset of Scrum to make the connections between the strategies used by software developers and those that faculty can adapt for academic research. Next, I will discuss strategies for constructing a solid foundation for teamwork, an often-overlooked aspect of collaborative research practices. This will include building a deeper understanding of managing a project backlog for a research team by looking at strategies for prioritizing and estimating stories. And finally the chapter will examine which Scrum strategies can be scaled to larger research programs with multiple researchers working on multiple concurrent projects.

Before continuing with this chapter, I highly recommend that you review the Scrum process as outlined in chapter 2 and the process adaptation for individual research described in chapter 3. This is the only chapter in the book dependent on other chapters, but taken as a whole, these three chapters will provide the foundation needed to implement Scrum in any academic research environment.

## Understanding the Foundations of Collaboration

When you think about working with a group, do you think about cooperating toward a common goal, the product being the sum of your collective efforts? Or do you think about collaborating, in which all team members are fully invested in the project, constantly interacting and debating, and creating a final product better than anything that could be accomplished individually? Hopefully when embarking on collaborative research, every member of the team believes that the combination of efforts will outshine individual work and make a greater contribution to knowledge.

Extensive research has been conducted about why organizational teams succeed or fail. Harvard Business School professor Morton Hansen (2009), who has studied collaboration within organizational units for more than a decade, asks a provocative question relevant to academic research teams: "Should we be surprised that collaboration fails in environments that are designed for . . . competition and independence? Of course not" (p. 11). Within environments that promote individual achievement, such as a promotion and tenure system and the emphasis by some accrediting bodies on single-author papers and grant funding, some faculty may have developed an aversion to collaboration that compounds problems within our teams.

Members of successful teams, on the other hand, share a set of common characteristics. After decades of work building productive teams, Jeff Sutherland (2014) argues that the best teams have every skill set and knowledge base needed to successfully complete a project from start to finish (p. 53). He and other collaboration researchers posit that successful teams

are driven by an unwavering commitment to a powerful goal and a united purpose;

agree upon a process and hold each other accountable throughout the work while being both unselfish and autonomous;

listen carefully to each member and build joint ideas through constructive debate and negotiation;

communicate regularly, honestly, and openly about progress, successes, failures, and needs;

are transparent in all their efforts within and across teams, understanding that there should be no hoarding of knowledge when everyone shares the same goals; and

maintain a positive, equitable, respectful attitude toward each other throughout the project (Cohn & Kearns, 2008; Gostick & Elton, 2010; Hansen, 2009; Riggio, 2013; Sawyer, 2007; Sutherland, 2014).

These characteristics are present in the best Scrum teams, as well. Agilist Prasad Prabhakaran (2010) argues that

> for any Agile project to be successful and hyper-productive, the team needs to show *more enthusiasm* and the right attitude towards *learning from peers* in spite of seniority and expertise. A *safety net* for fearless expression needs to be ensured so that *real camaraderie* can be exhibited, which in turn will increase focus on the goals of the team rather than "what is in it for me?" (para. 16, emphasis in original).

Camaraderie and trust are the foundations of a Scrum team, given the values that govern Agile as an ideology. Within these ideals, Mike Cohn and Martin Kearns (2008) acknowledge that the strongest team members want the best for the project and the team regardless of personal agendas or biases. These team members prefer to work collaboratively to identify and solve problems rather than seeking individual praise. Yet in a software environment, as in some academic environments, teamwork can be hamstrung by an unproductive focus on one or two star performers who have knowledge and skills that others may not.

Many Agile authors make the argument that the team must supersede the "rock star" team member because rock stars do not play well with others, unlike studio or jazz musicians, to use Ilan Goldstein's metaphor (2014, p. 22). Rock star egos damage the collaborative attitude of the team, with Goldstein (2012) commenting, "A group of brilliant yet egotistical individuals will never work as well as a group of solid yet collaborative teammates" (para. 19). By practicing the characteristics of good collaborators listed above and carefully avoiding the rock star mentality, faculty can build a strong foundation for research when working in Agile research teams.

### Department Chairs

Does your department function as a team? Could your department members collaborate on scholarly research? Consider how you might leverage some of the work you are already doing in departmental committees—curriculum innovation or assessment, for example—to encourage your peers to team up for publications or presentations. You might hold a workshop introducing some of these Scrum strategies and characteristics of an excellent team member to kick off the collaborations.

## Laying the Groundwork for Good Scrum Research Teams

One of the most often overlooked aspects of teamwork is the foundation. As faculty, we might join a lab already in progress, decide to work on something with a few graduate school friends, or invite some students into an active project. But how often do we take the time to articulate shared goals, rules of team behavior, roles to be covered, and commitments to each other as colleagues and co-researchers? What follows are some specific steps borrowed from Scrum trainers and Agile coaches to help kick off the research collaboration successfully.

## Who, and How Many?

Agile trainers and consultants who help organizations implement Agile spend time up-front creating, structuring, and empowering teams. Agile teams in industry are cross-functional and include each specialist needed to complete a piece of software functionality; therefore, mixing skills is just as important as mixing the right attitudes. Agile trainer and author Mike Cohn (2010) argues that the best Scrum teams have members from different areas, skill levels, and expertise; knowledge needed for the project; and diverse backgrounds and ways of problem solving (p. 190).

Creating cohesion and respect is crucial for Scrum teams because "teams succeed together and fail together. There is no 'my work' and 'your work' on a Scrum team, only 'our work'" (Cohn, 2010, p. 201). Part of being able to lay this groundwork is choosing not only the right people for the team but also the right number of people (p. 190). Group size should match the task, but we have all been on project teams that, for whatever reason, were too small or too big for the task at hand. What is optimal group size and composition?

Two measures are consistently used in Agile literature to define ideal Scrum teams: 7 +/− 2, or two pizzas. The first measure, five to nine people, seems to be based on the number of professionals with specialized development skills required for the team to be truly cross-functional and independent. The second measure is borrowed from Amazon.com, where teams are never bigger than could be fed by two pizzas for lunch (Cohn, 2010, p. 178). On a collaborative Agile research project, make sure that every member brings something unique and valuable to the project in terms of skills, knowledge, context, and approach and is willing to learn something from the other members in pursuit of the shared goal.

Smaller groups may have an easier time coordinating schedules, navigating group dynamics, and staying in constant communication; larger groups might have the advantage in generating more creative innovations when more constructive voices contribute. These numbers can also be used to scale up to much larger projects. Most software development projects have numerous teams working on different aspects of the application, each individual team composed of five to nine skilled professionals. The same strategy can be used for large research projects, as we'll discuss in a later section.

## How Will You Work Together?

One reason many collaborations become frustrating is that team members do not take the time at the beginning of a project to establish shared goals, collective commitments, and guidelines for team behavior. This can be as true for academic research teams as it is for software development teams or students working on a group project. But this important step can bring the team from a collection of individuals to a "we." Set aside time, perhaps on campus, at a conference, or via Skype if you are widely distributed, to work out the foundations of the team before moving forward with the project. Consider following this advice from Agile coach Lyssa Adkins (2010):

> Learning about the team starts with learning about each individual on the team and, from there, creating a shared team identity. . . .

Plan activities that allow the team members to relate to one another on a human level wherein they discover each other's skills, talents, and anything else they bring that will help achieve the goals of the work scheduled. (p. 150)

Many Agile teams call this activity "sprint 0" and will often hold a day-long team retreat to complete the sprint. If a retreat is not possible, dedicate at least an hour or two to do the following as a team:

**Share personal goals, competing priorities, and intended commitments.** Often when faculty agree to a group research project, especially in the excitement of doing interesting work with people we like and respect, we might not think through the ways in which it fits with our existing commitments. Have a discussion with the team at the beginning about what each person's priorities are, what commitments might interfere with participation on the project, and how much time and effort can be committed individually at that moment. From this discussion, make informed decisions about who might lead at different stages, what roles each member might play, and how to best work together to achieve the collective goal.

**Understand each other's strengths and weaknesses.** As academics, we should be able to acknowledge where our strengths lie and in what areas we can learn from our peers. Scrum requires open communication and respect between team members, which, while potentially difficult at first, provides a rich opportunity to acknowledge areas for professional growth and learning. One way to introduce this discussion is to complete a competency matrix activity as a team. As a team, begin by developing a list of "competencies" or skills you all agree are important to the research you are undertaking. Make each of these competencies a row in a spreadsheet. Along the other axis, assign each person a column. Each person then adds an "*" to competencies they have expertise in, an "&" to those about which they are interested in learning more, and a "−" to those with which they have

TABLE 4.1  Sample competency matrix

|  | Dr. A | Dr. B | Dr. C | Dr. D |
|---|---|---|---|---|
| Activity theory | * | & | & | – |
| Actor network theory | * | & | – | & |
| Survey methods | – | * | – | & |
| Ethnographic observation | – | – | * |  |
| Data coding/ Grounded theory | & | * | & | * |
| Etc. |  |  |  |  |

less experience (see table 4.1 for a completed matrix). This activity allows team members to self-reflect, share their competencies with the team, ensure the necessary skills are present, and articulate how team members can learn from each other.

**Determine shared goals for the research.** Teams who do not articulate goals for the project clearly and early are more likely to experience negative group dynamics and unsatisfying products later. What impact do you intend to make on the discipline or community with the research? How does the research fit into everyone's personal goals and agendas? What meaningful outcomes does the team expect to achieve—a presentation, workshop, article, book, public report, or some combination? What is the target journal or publisher? Establishing these goals early in the process and revisiting them regularly can help the team make good decisions in the long run.

**Agree on expectations and behaviors.** Once you have shared priorities and established collective goals, develop a working contract for the research team. This might seem like an unnecessary step, especially if you are working with friends or trusted colleagues, but rules created at the outset of the project can be used to deal with awkward issues that might arise later. Develop guidelines for the acceptable baseline of participation, make a commitment to using the Scrum process, and agree on ways to address conflict constructively. Ideally, the guidelines will not be needed, but it never hurts to have a plan in place for dealing with issues that might arise and affect the work.

**Agree on all logistics.** This step is crucial, especially if your group is distributed across locations. Establish a time to meet every one to two weeks, and agree to hold that time sacred on your calendars. Establishing this commitment early allows team members to block it out on their calendars for an extended period and will help the project stay on everyone's radar. Agree on what tools and methods will be used, how to share and version data, how to communicate outside of scheduled meetings, what means of contact to use, etc.

Post your group rules where everyone has access to them. Establishing these foundations early adds another layer of trust and commitment among team members that can inform the success of the team for the rest of the project. Once the team is in place and structured appropriately, begin to develop the backlog of stories and tasks that will guide the project(s) (see chapter 3).

### New Faculty

If you are just joining an established research team, consider asking your fellow researchers to hold a sprint 0 planning meeting in the interest of socializing you as a member of the team and reviewing current processes for any potential areas of improvement.

Taking time to lay groundwork for professional research relationships before starting projects provides a solid foundation for interactions that can ease collaboration throughout the work. The next section explores how teams can use the backlog effectively to manage the projects as they kick off the collaboration.

## Prioritizing, Estimating, and Visualizing the Research Backlog

The next step in laying the foundation for a successful Scrum research team is to build the project backlog. Chapters 2 and 3 cover how to create a backlog using epics and stories, so this section focuses on the collaborative aspects of the process, specifically prioritizing and estimating backlog stories.

### Prioritizing with a Product Owner

As discussed in chapter 2, the backlog is "owned" by a person in the role of product owner, or the PO. The PO is the link between the software development teams and the business side, both of whom have a stake in what gets built, when, and in what order. One of the primary duties of the PO is to prioritize the backlog of stories that the teams will eventually complete based on insider knowledge of what stakeholders want at different times in the project. The PO prioritizes the stories based on a number of criteria such as logical next steps, pieces that must be completed before other stories can be done (dependencies), functionality the stakeholder needs more urgently, etc. Because the backlog is a working document, the PO regularly adds and removes stories as the project continues, making sure each story is detailed enough for the team to understand, for the most part, what is expected of them and what will constitute successful completion of the story (acceptance criteria or "definition of done").

In software Scrum teams, the PO is technically a member of the team but with a role unlike that of the other members: to work closely with the team to flesh out stories and make sure the most valuable work on the backlog is being completed every sprint. However, having a member in an academic research team serve as a PO can add value by allowing one person to coordinate the backlog and keep members focused on the priorities of the project.

Large research teams with multiple projects in play might be able to easily identify a PO, perhaps a lab manager, project coordinator, or principal investigator. For these large, complex projects, having a third party who is aware of each aspect of in-progress research activities can make maintaining the backlog across the program or lab much easier. Small, single project research teams can benefit from identifying a PO for the project; a team member who is organized and detail oriented can help everyone see both the immediate and long-term activities to be done based on collective goals. A team member with these skills might self-identify during team planning activities, or the team might ask for a volunteer to manage the backlog for the group.

In either scenario, the PO for the team takes responsibility for staying apprised of everyone's work, updating the stories in the backlog, and sharing that work with the team during sprint planning. If there are multiple projects under one umbrella, POs are charged with staying connected to the work of other teams and how it might impact their own team. Using this knowledge, they can adjust team priorities and backlog items as needed. POs are important components of the Scrum process as they help the team maintain the integrity of the backlog and stay on track toward joint goals.

## Estimating Backlog Stories

Humans are notoriously bad at estimating how much time an activity will take. But effective estimation is an important skill for a team, especially a faculty research team, when schedules can be at cross-purposes and available blocks of time for research scattered. Taking time to collectively estimate the stories associated with the research plans will help to give the team a much better sense of commitments and the effort required to be successful. Working with the backlog can be more complicated when more voices want to be heard, but collaborative backlog construction often generates better ideas and stories (chapter 3).

For teams, estimating how long a story will take or how much effort it will require is a learned skill; over time and several sprints, they discover how much they can realistically complete together per sprint, or their "velocity." An estimate is not a commitment but rather an educated guess based on available information about each story at the time. That estimate might be thrown off when new information comes to light, and with this information the PO can adjust the backlog as necessary. Spending the time to estimate during the sprint planning session helps the team to control their time and hopefully overcome Parkinson's Law: work expands to fill the time available for its completion.

Estimating in terms of time is the common, but not necessarily the most effective, metric in the case of large projects; other metrics such as complexity and "bigness" of the story can be more useful in this context. Thinking with a Scrum perspective means moving away from a standard linear perception of time to a more holistic and cyclical understanding, which helps team members rethink how to productively estimate tasks (Sutherland, 2014, p. 81). Scrum teams have different strategies for estimating the effort stories on the backlog will require, ranging from the abstract such as T-shirt sizing and story points to more specific such as ideal or actual hours (Ashmore & Runyon, 2014, pp. 155–156). When using ideal vs. actual hours, for example, members of the team estimate how many hours a task or story will take ideally then map that time onto their workload for actual hours. A team member might estimate that a certain story would take eight ideal hours of dedicated work but in conjunction with other work and commitments the story may take two weeks to finish in actual time.

T-shirt sizing and story points are detailed below and can be useful for academic research teams estimating backlog items because these strategies effectively remove traditional time-based estimating faculty may be used to and impose a new way of thinking about complexity.

*Estimating with T-shirt Sizing*
Think about standard T-shirt sizes: a small shirt is relatively smaller than a medium but not exponentially smaller, and so on through the sizes of shirts. When using T-shirt sizes as an abstract estimation tool, the goal is to match the size of the story to the size of a T-shirt (Goldstein, 2014, p. 70). Pick your scale—perhaps S–L or XS–XL—and work together to assign each story a size based not only on the time you think it will take to complete but also on the complexity of the story and number of tasks required. For example, completing a literature review might be an L or an XL, while gaining IRB approval for a survey study might be a S (see figure 4.1). By assigning a T-shirt size to the stories for each sprint, the team begins to develop norms about the extent of work to be done, rather than the time it might take, so that the best decisions

**Story: IRB      Story: Lit Review**
**8 points       32 points**

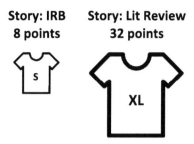

Fig. 4.1 Using T-shirt sizing and story points to estimate stories

can be made about what to commit to during a sprint. The likelihood of completing two XL stories in a two-week sprint might be very low, but two medium stories might be doable.

*Estimating with Story Points*
Story points is an abstract estimating activity that uses a scale, such as powers of two, to determine the level of effort required to complete stories (Ashmore & Runyon, 2014, pp. 156–159). With this system, stories are assigned a number of "points" relative to their perceived size. For example, using the power of two scale, you would assign each story one of the following: 2, 4, 8, 16, 32, or 64 (Rubin, 2013, p. 130). The numbers allow the team to see the complexity of stories without assigning hour estimates. Teams that have been working together for a while might understand that their productive capacity for a sprint is 32 points, indicating that they should take on only stories that add up to 32 and that a story worth 64 points should probably be broken down into smaller stories (see figure 4.1). Using the previous example, the lit review might be worth 32, while the IRB application, only 8.

Department Chairs and Program Coordinators

Consider holding a workshop for your faculty that raises issues related to collaborative research, prioritizing, and estimating. Sharing these strategies and leading faculty through related activities may help those who are struggling with project management or who are looking for new ways to better understand their existing work commitments.

## Estimating in Practice

To conduct a productive estimating session with your research team,

**Make estimating a regular part of your sprint planning meetings.** The more often a team estimates, the more likely the team is to formulate to a group norm, which will speed up the process even more.

**Work from the prioritized backlog.** Select the top stories from the prioritized Scrum backlog to work on during the sprint. Scrum teams will often estimate a few stories beyond what can reasonably be completed during one sprint just so they have a sense of what is coming next.

**Use a combination of private and group estimation.** When a story is up for estimation, have each member of the team write down individual estimates first so as not to be influenced by others. Then have everyone hold up their estimations. If everyone is close, you can move on. If they vary widely, start a time-limited group discussion as to why members think the story is the size they voted. One way to control this conversation is to have the person who voted highest debate the person who voted lowest until they come to a compromise.

**Strive for consensus.** Allow team members to have their say in estimation, but consider the opinion of the person who might be most responsible for that particular story since he or she will have a better sense of how complex the story really is. If consensus seems a long way off, discuss how the story might be broken down further or what it is that is driving the disagreement (someone might have some knowledge that the rest of the team needs to best understand the story).

**Convert to hours if necessary.** If the team is sprinting and committed to completing specific stories in a certain time frame, you might be comfortable with the relative estimates you have reached via consensus. But it can also be helpful to convert the story from a relative estimate to an ideal/actual time estimate to get a stronger sense of how many people should be assigned a story and how to move forward.

Over time, teams will develop the ability to accurately estimate how much effort a story or task will take based on their understanding of their own work productivity (capacity) and their average rate of work (velocity). Taking the time to estimate, especially for new teams, helps to set goals and commitments that team members can strive to achieve for the good of the research. Equally important is visualizing the goals so that progress can be celebrated and delays or problems addressed immediately. To facilitate this process, set up a Scrum board in an easily accessible place, and use it regularly. See chapter 2 to learn how to set up a physical Scrum board. If a digital board is more appropriate for your team, there are several software packages that can be used to manage Scrum-based projects, including LeanKit, VersionOne, and Basecamp.

This section covered backlog management for single research teams, like the nurses in the introductory example. But managing a backlog across a large project with multiple teams can be more challenging. This is certainly an issue most Agile organizations face; virtually all software projects have multiple teams working on different features, and many run teams with members distributed across the world. The next section introduces strategies for scaling the backlog and sprint process for multi-team projects, such as the one described in the biochemist example at the beginning of this chapter.

### Scaling the Backlog across Multiple Teams

Scrum was created to guide large projects with multiple teams working on different aspects of a software program, so the framework transfers very well to large research programs that consist of multiple concurrent projects. The plan-execute-reflect Scrum loop is perfect for teams within larger systems. Here are some tips that can be used to scale Scrum to a large research program:

Reconsider the backlog itself. A typical rule of thumb for software projects is "one product, one backlog," but this rule might not map very well to research when we do not necessarily think of our work as "products" (Cohn, 2010, p. 330). It is important to keep the backlog manageable for all the teams working on the program or larger project. One way to do that is to have one overarching program backlog that consists of the epics that teams are working on rather than the individual stories within the epics (p. 322). Teams then have smaller project backlogs connected to the program backlog, which breaks out the epics into clearer stories and tasks. Many of the available enterprise-level Scrum software tools will let you build multiple levels into the project so that each team's work is accessible to the whole project team but not overwhelming at a glance.

Choose an appropriate product owner structure. Who manages the backlog is an important decision for multi-team projects. In a traditional sense, one PO should have the power to maintain the overall backlog for the entire research program. For projects with many interdependencies, that might work very well. But for really large projects, that backlog may quickly become unwieldy. In this case, consider having one primary PO and other POs dedicated to two or three teams. The team POs might be graduate students reporting to the main PO or representatives from each team who work together to maintain and prioritize the overarching program backlog (Cohn, 2010, p. 328). The POs can determine how best to visualize the shared backlogs to ensure transparency across teams.

Use daily Scrum, Scrum of Scrums, and Scrum ambassadors. Scrum teams in industry are usually working concurrently with other teams on different pieces of the same application. Using Scrum of Scrums or Scrum ambassadors, teams connect, share solutions, and learn from each other. To apply this adaptation to your research program, first make every effort possible to have individual teams working on similar sprint schedules (Cohn, 2010, p. 344). Then have each team hold regular daily Scrums (or whatever interval is most effective depending on when people are together). If teams use the Scrum of Scrums meeting format, each team then sends a representative, usually the Scrum Master or a senior team member, to a second Scrum with other team representatives who share progress and concerns across teams (Rubin, 2013, pp. 218–220). The representatives report back useful information to their teams. Another option is what Ilan Goldstein (2014) calls Scrum ambassadors. Using this approach, each team sends a representative to other teams' Scrums to listen and add relevant information from his or her team as necessary (p. 109). Team ambassadors then share the information learned with their teams. Both approaches can have advantages and disadvantages, but both keep the teams connected and aware of the work others are doing toward the same overarching goals.

**Consider using an Agile-specific software package if your team is distributed across locations.** Since a physical Scrum board is not an option for distributed teams, collaborative software is a good alternative for visualizing work collectively. While I do not endorse or recommend these specifically, software packages such as those offered by LeanKit, VersionOne, and Trello all offer academic versions and differently scalable packages depending on the size of the project and number of users. Basecamp, with some additional programming, can also be adapted to be used for Scrum projects.

**Hold sprint reviews.** The review meeting that closes the sprint is an important part of the Scrum loop, requiring the team to demonstrate what they have completed during the sprint. If research teams are working on the same sprint schedule, a specific time can be set aside at the end of the sprint to allow each team to present to the other teams. This could take a variety of forms, from write-ups to visual demos to discussions, depending on what works best for your researchers. Holding regular review meetings allows each team to see what the other teams are doing and learning and to perhaps contribute a solution to a problem or find a new idea that benefits another project. This can also help remind everyone that they are one large team working toward collective goals.

**Introduce modified retrospectives.** I recommend that individual teams gather for retrospectives—discussions among themselves about what went well and what can be improved in terms of process—after their sprint reviews. But also consider having a retrospective meeting of senior representatives from each team. Ask them to write team strengths and areas for improvement on individual sticky notes (Goldstein, 2014, pp. 125–126). On a white board draw a continuum with "needs work" and "good" at the poles and "OK" in the middle. Instruct the representatives to position sticky note points along the continuum. Then work together to group similar items, discuss them, and decide what each representative will take back to the teams in terms of shared successes and practices to improve. Doing a modified retrospective such as this in addition to the individual retrospectives can help teams stay connected and committed to improvement across the research program.

Managing large-scale research programs is complex and difficult, especially for researchers not trained in any type of formal project management. These tips for scaling Scrum practices can be useful for creating cohesion, supporting connections across smaller projects, and helping everyone remember the larger goals and resources of the program.

### Department Chairs and Program Coordinators

If your department or program has multiple committees working toward different aspects of your joint goals, you might consider adapting the Scrum of Scrums meeting or using Scrum ambassadors to make sure these teams are communicating clearly with each other and you.

## Wrapping Up

In this chapter, we examined different Scrum strategies that can be used to manage collaborative research projects. Every project is different, and not every strategy will work in each context. However, implementing a few of these strategies in your projects can improve your research collaborations in productive ways.

In addition to research, faculty spend a good deal of time in service commitments to student organizations, university committees, disciplinary organizations, and the community. The next chapters explore Scrum strategies within the context of faculty service, beginning with committee work.

# 5

# Leading Effective Agile Committees

After reading this chapter, you will be able to

- Understand the relationship between Agile and servant leadership
- Launch a new committee or task force using a Scrum team kick-off approach
- Deal with common committee-related productivity and people issues using Agile facilitation

Putting people into groups isn't a magical dust that makes everyone more creative. It has to be the right kind of group, and the group has to match the nature of the task.
—Keith Sawyer, *Group Genius: The Creative Power of Collaboration*

Most meetings suck.
—Laura Burke, "A Culture of Great Meetings"

How many times have you looked at your calendar for the week to see committee meeting after committee meeting lined up? How many of those meetings have you been excited to attend? Committees and service are one part of the three-legged stool that constitutes faculty work. We serve our institutions, disciplines, and communities by providing our skills and time. Our committees advance important goals through collaborative work, understanding that representative participation from across campus or college encourages the best approaches to problems and opportunities. This is especially true when committee members trust and respect each other's commitment to shared goals and expend equitable levels of energy, firm in the belief that they are representing the best interests of the institution and their peers.

However, we all too often find ourselves on ill-conceived or poorly run committees thinking that we could have accomplished via email what we just spent an hour arguing about in person. Committees with clear shared goals and committed members still can suffer from a lack of an agreed-upon process or conflicting ideas about how to reach those goals. Even the best committees can be frustrating when members cannot agree on fundamental roles, goals, and purposes for working together.

Underlying Scrum practices, as articulated in the Agile values, is a "fundamental belief that, given a simple framework, small groups of people can achieve great things together" (Adkins, 2010, p. 96). Many cross-disciplinary committees and special task forces, especially those charged with making difficult decisions or exploring complex issues, can benefit from the organizing practices of Scrum and team facilitation techniques used by Agile coaches. I have not yet come across faculty committees using Agile to manage their work, so what follows covers potentially new territory. I believe that Agile team strategies and a Scrum framework can transfer well into faculty committee environments because committees are similar in form and function to cross-functional teams in industry.

In this chapter, I will explore how faculty can put Agile and Scrum practices into action to lead strong faculty committees. To get started, I will first briefly discuss how the concept of servant leadership is relevant to Agile, then cover how to use Scrum to launch a successful committee and deal with potential blockers to effective committee work.

## Serving as an Agile Leader

Though most Agile practitioners strive for flat hierarchies and value the contributions of every team member, proponents are also aware that the best teams require some level of support and facilitation to keep them on track, learning, and working well together. Agile leaders are not traditional, command-and-control managers. On the contrary, Jeff Sutherland (2014) built the Scrum roles with the mindset that leadership and authority are not the same thing (p. 177). The best way to describe the Agile leadership mindset is to align it with Robert K. Greenleaf's concept of servant leadership. Greenleaf's servant leaders are deeply concerned for the personal and professional development of each person in the community or organization they serve. Rather than focus on cultivating wealth and power for themselves, servant leaders focus on cultivating shared power, encouraging collaboration, respecting each person, and making sure people have meaningful work to do (Greenleaf, n.d.; Hess, 2013).

All team members, therefore, can serve as situational leaders to the team as needed. But within the flat Agile hierarchy, the product owner (PO), Scrum Master, and coach serve more formalized roles. As outlined in chapter 2, the PO is the interface between the business and the team and is responsible for accurately maintaining the project backlog. The Scrum Master is the team facilitator, committed to supporting the growth and development of the team. And the Agile coach is charged with inspiring team members to be their best in any situation. People in each of these roles are servant leaders within the Agile structure.

Agile servant leaders believe in the potential and power of the team. They create environments in which the team can work, learn, reflect, and grow while achieving consistent productivity and continuous improvement. They are communicative and collaborative. They allow teams to self-organize, support their work, help the team learn from failures, and keep the team accountable to commitments. They are motivators of people, knowledgeable about the Agile framework being used and the individuals within a team. They share the characteristics of collaborative leaders, who, as described by Harvard collaboration expert Morton Hansen (2009) strive to "create a unifying goal, incite a common value of teamwork, and speak the language of collaboration" by involving others in all decisions, seeking common ground, and "redefining success" with the team and organization (pp. 74, 147, 151). Agile servant leaders are facilitators, champions, and team players (Roriz Filho, 2011; Saddington, 2011; Scrum Mastering, 2014).

Faculty committee chairs are servant leaders as well. When we think of committees as teams of respected peers who bring valuable skills to the table and who share a commitment to serving via this work, we refresh our leadership with an Agile perspective. No one loves to sit in unproductive meetings, and approaching committee work from an Agile perspective is one way faculty can change the process to encourage productive work from committee members in a new way.

### Department Chairs

Think about how you are using or can use this leadership style to create teams in your department. These teams can take ownership of important department work such as assessment, curriculum, and long-term planning, especially when composed of members across department areas and lines. This strategy puts you in the role of product owner, maintaining the goals of the department while guiding the committee priorities and delegating work.

### Launching (or Resetting) the Agile Faculty Committee

How are most committees formed? At my institution, the head of the academic council sends a request for committee preferences to the faculty. Using those responses, a subgroup of council members (a committee on committees, if you will), assigns membership based on those requests. Ad hoc committees or special task forces are usually appointed by the dean or provost based on knowledge of each faculty member's skills and interests. Yet, as Keith Sawyer implies in the quote that introduced this chapter, successful collaboration does not begin at formation but must be built.

When an organization chooses to implement an Agile process such as Scrum, trained experts are often brought in to help build teams and educate people on the process. While we might eventually get to the place where we have Agile higher education consultants who can help faculty launch Scrum-style committees, for now faculty leaders can use Agile team strategies to kick off productive committees. These strategies can also be used to reset a committee at the start of new academic year to make sure everyone is on the same page with goals and process.

## Pick the Right People

The first order of business is to select the right people for the job at hand whenever possible. Agile teams in industry are cross-functional, bringing expertise from all areas necessary to build, test, and complete working software during sprints. A good academic committee or task force is no different. At an institutional level, it might be useful to have faculty submit a short list of skills, passions, and expertise they can contribute to different committee appointments rather than just a committee preference list. Dean- and provost-level committees are likely formed using this information tacitly, but having it on paper can help the people forming the team make the best decisions for a well-balanced and dedicated committee. Chairs can use this information to create functional internal committees to do the work of the department. While personalities and temperaments are certainly worth taking into account, the best teams benefit from constructive conflict, so choose individuals who have the best combination of skills, are comfortable negotiating common ground, and will respect peers throughout the process.

Consider committee size as well. While some committees, such as a university-wide curriculum committee, will likely require representation from across campus, what is the optimal size of a committee to maximize time, encourage active engagement, and ensure outcomes? The general rule of thumb for appropriate group size for Agile teams is 7 $+/-$ 2, which allows optimal communication and coordination, constructive interactions, fewer social loafers, higher participation, and greater ultimate satisfaction in the job done (Hartman, 2012, p. 12.2; Cohn, 2010, p. 179). For example, a task force might include nine people, a standing committee, seven, and a department committee, five.

Addressing these factors can help to create a committee with an appropriately diverse set of skills and knowledge and who are poised to collaborate and produce good work. Of course, committee selection is not always in our hands, so the next set of strategies can be used to help the committee members gel and develop a level of trust necessary for successful collaborative work.

## Hold a Committee Retreat

When introducing Scrum to an organization, many Agile coaches prefer to hold a retreat to launch new teams. Agile industry retreats might last one or two days, depending on the complexity of the team's task, and would include an array of team-building activities, Scrum-process training, project-backlog planning, and first-sprint planning. One Agile coach, for example, has "found that having all the 'conversations' in one room empowered the participants to make more decisions in one day than they could have in three months of endless emails and smaller meetings" (Kilby, 2013, p. 101). Whether onsite or off, retreats allow teams and leaders to focus, commit to the process, and build respect.

Consider holding a committee planning retreat at the end of the academic year or a week or two before the new year begins. Retreat length would depend on the committee and its charges: a Friday afternoon early in the semester, a day in the summer, or an off-site weekend with an associated stipend all provide concentrated time to focus. Yes, faculty will likely balk at the extra time required, but giving a group time to focus on collaboration and the work at hand before they will otherwise be pulled in numerous directions can be invaluable for setting the tone for the future. Food or a promised post-retreat happy hour never hurt either.

What do you do at an Agile committee retreat? I recommend four types of activities: team building, committee charter development, goal setting and initial backlog building, and finally sprint planning.

*Team Building*

Most people cringe at the words "team building," but Scrum teams are built on the foundations of the Agile values: focus, courage, commitment, respect, and openness. As such, Agile coach and author Lyssa Adkins says that productive team building activities "help people learn about one another so they can depend on each other as they pursue shared goals. No fluffy stuff here" (Adkins, 2010, p. 150). Committee leaders can guide the group in an activity or two to form early bonds of trust and seed collaboration. These strategies can work for members who already know each other but might not be familiar with each other's skills in this context, as well as with new groups or new members:

**Competency matrix.** (See chapter 4.) Start by having each person compile a list of skills or competencies they think will be important to completing the work of the committee (Laestadius, 2012). Put the lists on a white board. As a group, compare notes, and develop a shared list of competencies needed to be successful. Next, make each competency a row in a grid. Along the other axis, assign each person a column, and ask them to add an asterisk next to competencies in which they have expertise, an ampersand next to those about which they are interested in learning more, and a dash next to those with which they have limited or no expertise. Use this self-reflective activity to discuss how each person can uniquely contribute to the committee work. Through this exercise, the team members learn more about each other and build a foundation of trust and respect for their work to come.

**Marketplace of skills.** This activity works well for a creative group and requires large sticky notes (20" × 30"), different colored markers, and wall space. The purpose of the activity is to allow each committee member to illustrate the skills, knowledge, abilities, and interests they bring to the committee. Each person draws their own "stall" in the committee's skills marketplace to showcase these competencies. Members then "explore the market," making notes on a set of smaller sticky notes that they add to the posters—green for competencies that are exciting, red for competencies the person has but did not list, and yellow for competencies other members can help the person develop. The group can then discuss each poster and how to integrate that person's competencies into the overall committee team (Laestadius, 2012; Adkins, 2010, pp. 153–154).

**Pre-mortem.** Faculty tend to be pragmatic people who have likely experienced bad committees in the past, so this exercise allows members to get their concerns out on the table early in the process. Have each member individually brainstorm the answer to the questions "What will go wrong?" and "How will this end in disaster?" Depending on how comfortable members of the group are with each other, the concerns might be written on cards and shared anonymously, or an open discussion can begin. While perhaps dramatic, the questions and resulting discussion surface both process and product concerns that the team can plan around in the team charter (Gray, Brown & Macanufo, 2010, p. 117).

**"I don't like/I like."** This strategy helps the team develop the behavioral rules for the committee and can be a lively activity or a simple discussion, depending on the spirit of the group. In the lively version, give each person an index card, and ask them to complete the sentence, "I don't like it when . . ." in reference to committee work. Then collect the cards, shuffle them, and give a randomly selected card to each person. Ask all members to read their new card and to write an inverse statement on the back: "I like when. . . ." Repeat the process one or two more times. Use the cards to start a discussion about positive and negative team behaviors. You can have the same discussion without the cards, asking each person to share their best and worst committee experiences, then turning those into statements about good team work and collaboration strategies. This discussion can help members understand each other's approaches to collaboration and develop shared commitments to process and respect.

Using one or two of these strategies at a committee retreat helps members get to know one another better and begin to build trust. Adkins acknowledges that adults are sometimes reluctant to engage in what they might consider icebreakers or silly get-to-know-you activities. If this is the case with your committee, she recommends explaining the purpose of the activity, how long you plan to spend on it, and what you expect at least one positive outcome of the activity will be, just as you would do when introducing an activity with students (pp. 154–155).

*Committee Charter Development*
If you used the "I don't like/I like" activity as a team builder, you will likely have a list of behaviors that the group can prioritize and agree to follow as a committee. These can be codified into a committee charter document that articulates the rules of engagement, so to speak, for the committee's tenure together. Good charters for Agile teams include a clear statement of the team's goals and expected behaviors. The charter might include guidelines for how to communicate with each other within and outside of meetings, expectations about time commitments for each member, specifics about when and where meetings will be and how long a sprint will be, a clear articulation of the team process, an agreed-upon method of achieving consensus, and a specific plan for managing conflict that arises. This can be done as a large group or in small groups who suggest guidelines for different parts of the charter. Once the committee has reached a consensus, type up the charter, and put it in a shared online space for reference as needed.

If the committee did not use the "I don't like/I like" activity, start the charter discussion by asking committee members to share, first, their worst committee experiences and then their best experiences. Ask the person sharing an experience to articulate what made that experience so bad or so good in one clear statement, which you write on a board or in a shared document. For example, a member might share a bad experience in which the committee failed in part because no one responded to the committee chair's emails. From this, the member might articulate that methods of communication must be clearly defined and agreed upon before the work begins. Use the list of behaviors developed to create agreements for the committee charter. In this example, a committee guideline might then be that committee members agree to respond to committee-related emails within 24 hours.

Collaboration researcher Morten Hansen (2009) poses an important question that teams should ask themselves while defining behaviors: "How do we cultivate collaboration in the right way so that we achieve the great things that are not possible when we are divided?" (p. 3). These team building and committee charter activities are just a few that can be used to help members create a foundation for achieving those "great things" while working together effectively.

### Department Chairs

Consider using your department retreat early in the semester, at least in part, to set yearly goals and to do some productive team building. This can help build relationships and trust among faculty in different areas and enculturate new members to the department. These activities would work at the level of the entire department or in department committees, depending on group size.

### Goal Setting and Backlog Generating

Whether it be a faculty committee, a Scrum team, or a student group working on a project, the most successful collaborations are built on a shared commitment to specific goals. For many faculty committees, goals are stated in the charge from the provost, dean, or faculty handbook. While a special task force might have a more defined timeline and set of deliverables to create than a standing committee, all committees do valuable work toward institutional goals.

Understanding the committee charge is the first step in generating the committee backlog. Here are some steps for clearly articulating committee goals and creating the initial backlog:

1.  **Rearticulate the committee goals together.** In most cases, administration or faculty leadership sets the committee's charge, but the committee must determine how to effectively complete the charge (Sutherland, 2014, p. 50). As a committee, restate the goals from the charge in your own words, adding any additional goals you believe are necessary to accomplishing the main charge. Use the language of epics and stories so that you are creating backlog items simultaneously (chapter 2). For example, a task force might restate a charge to create a report on the state of support for LGBTQIA students on campus by a certain date as follows:

    *As faculty members who care deeply that all students are treated with dignity on campus, we want to create a detailed report on the status of existing services and support structures available on campus for LGBTQIA students by January 1 so that we can make better decisions in the spring about innovative policies for a safe, welcoming campus.*

    This epic could then be broken down into smaller stories and discrete tasks to be accomplished by the group.

2.  **Create and visualize the stories.** Starting with the epics developed from the committee charge, brainstorm stories that might be necessary to complete the epics. Write the stories the committee creates on sticky notes, and put them on a Scrum-designated wall, white board, or shared online document. As a team, evaluate each potential story within each epic, choose the most logical stories to complete, and prioritize those stories according to immediacy and complexity.

3.  **Determine consensus for stories if there is disagreement.** If all members of the committee do not agree on stories or priorities suggested, begin an honest conversation to reach a consensus. Manage the conversation as necessary, perhaps by setting a time

limit or allowing each member to make two statements during the session; discussion guidelines can be drawn from the committee charter. The Fist of Five strategy explained below can also be used, not to make sure everyone is in complete agreement, but to make sure that each member can say, "I understand, and I can live with this decision."

### Fist of Five Consensus Voting

When an opportunity for a vote or straw poll arises, use the Fist of Five strategy to take the pulse of the committee. Using this strategy, members vote with their hands after the leader makes a clear statement on which the vote will be taken. The following is a standard scale that can be used:

| | |
|---|---|
| Closed fist | I cannot and will never support it. |
| One finger | I don't support it. |
| Two fingers | I don't support it but am open to more discussion. |
| Three fingers | I understand and can live with it. |
| Four fingers | I support it. |
| Five fingers | I fully support it and will defend it to others. |

Fist of Five can be written into a team charter as a primary means of arriving at consensus. The committee might define its own scale and agree that a certain number of committee members must vote three fingers or higher to move forward. The committee might also define what would happen if votes are polarized. One strategy might be to give the members who voted the highest and the lowest time for a mini-debate to see if opinions can be swayed.

Many committees stumble because members understand the goals for the work differently. And some faculty members may come to the committee with personal biases or agendas that can slow down progress. By articulating the goals and the backlog as one team during a time set aside specifically for this work, committee members have the immediate opportunity to shape the goals (within reason) and be heard if concerns exist. And by going through this process, the team will have created a committee backlog from which to begin its work.

### First Sprint Planning

The time at the end of the first committee meeting should be spent planning the specific activities to be completed during the first sprint. (See chapter 2 for detailed coverage of sprints.) The committee might also think ahead a sprint or two to envision the possible flow of the work. Based on the team agreement about sprint length in the charter, determine as a group which epic or stories you will commit to working on between that moment and the next meeting. If tasks for the stories have not been broken out, do so now. Equitably distribute the tasks according to interest, time available, and skill sets. Agree upon how and when the committee members will report to each other during the sprint (e.g., Will each member check in on a certain day with an update to the committee? Are short written reports due to everyone before the next meeting? Will members give short reports to start the next meeting?). Once the sprint plan is in place, the work of the committee begins.

These strategies can be used to start a new committee, to refresh an existing one that could benefit from a new process, or to reset a committee that has taken on new members. While a goal in Agile is to keep teams together as long as possible, faculty governance policies typically require rotating representation on faculty committees, so these strategies can be valuable to start a new year with an important committee. But the real work of the committee, and the committee chair, starts after the retreat.

### Faculty Working with Community Partners

Consider using these strategies on any committee or project in your service activities, especially if you are working with members of the community. This preliminary work can build necessary trust and mutual commitment early in the process, encourage mutual engagement, and perhaps avoid perceived town-and-gown issues down the road.

## Facilitating the Agile Committee

As noted earlier, most Agile and Scrum advocates argue that Scrum teams don't have "leaders" but instead have a varied structure of mentors and facilitators whose task it is to help the teams achieve incremental, iterative, and continuous progress. Product owners focus on maintaining the backlog so that the team can focus attention on completing prioritized stories. Scrum Masters and Scrum coaches serve the team to ensure good process and individual professional development. But team members are also expected to assume situational authority when the opportunity arises.

Academic committee chairs can be product owners, Scrum Masters, and coaches at various times during their tenure with a committee. Agile chairs maintain and visualize the committee's backlog, facilitate committee discussions and decisions, work to remove external or internal blocks to progress, and hold committee members accountable to commitments. The committee chair helps the team develop an Agile process that allows them to be productive, constructive, and reflective. In the following section, I offer Agile strategies for three committee chair functions: setting meeting agendas, facilitating discussion, and managing conflict.

## Setting Meeting Agendas

The Scrum Master and product owner meet with the team at different stages of the sprint cycle, and team members can call meetings as necessary. The agenda for a daily Scrum meeting is always the same; team members respond to the three daily Scrum questions: What have I done since we last met? What will I do today? What impediments could potentially impede progress? Planning and retrospective meetings are facilitated by the product owner and Scrum Master, respectively. Because committee work is only one facet of an Agile faculty member's duties, it is conceivable that elements of all the Scrum meetings (daily Scrum, planning, review, and retrospective, see chapter 2) might occur in the committee's monthly or bi-monthly meeting.

Agenda setting is important for making sure these combination meetings stay on track and are productive. The following are two strategies you might use to set an agenda yourself or with the committee membership:

**7Ps.** The 7P strategy encourages reflection on seven elements before a meeting. Working quickly through these elements can help you prepare for the meeting holistically and specifically so that you can facilitate more effectively:

Purpose—What is the purpose of the meeting?

People—Who needs to be there, and why?

Product—What artifact will you create during the meeting?

Process—What are the items to be covered in the meeting to achieve the purpose?

Prep—What might committee members need to do before the meeting?

Pitfalls—What are the risks associated with the meeting, or what ground rules might need to be in place to ensure productivity?

Practical Concerns—When and where is the meeting? Will there be food? (Gray, Brown & Macanufo, 2010, pp. 54–55)

**Pie chart agenda.** With this strategy, you might complete a 7P analysis before the meeting and then determine how much attention to give each item to be covered. Present the agenda as a pie chart instead of a list. The committee uses the visual of a pie chart to give weight to each element you intend to cover in the meeting as well as any items the members feel are important to discuss as well (Gray, Brown & Macanufo, 2010, pp. 112–113).

## Facilitating Discussion

Scrum Masters and coaches use many strategies to facilitate team discussions, especially in retrospective meetings about team process and issue-related meetings outside of the usual Scrum rituals. A meeting facilitator's job is to help members to use the agreed-upon discussion process and offer observations and questions that move the discussion along. Scrum Masters and coaches are not considered team members in the same way that an academic chair is a functioning member of the committee, and faculty committee chairs are often trained in facilitating student discussions, a skill that translates directly to committee work. With that in mind, here are two simple facilitation strategies to add to your Agile toolkit:

**Use sprint reports and daily Scrum at the start of each meeting.** Because Scrum is designed to keep people accountable to each other for the work they have committed to, the process has built-in checks to ensure everyone is meeting individual commitments. Consider having committee members submit a very brief report before the meeting that can be compiled and shared with the entire committee for a snapshot of team progress. Similarly, if you hold a variation of a daily Scrum at the beginning of each committee meeting, limiting each person to report on what they have accomplished and what they might need assistance with, you make accountability public to the committee at every meeting. Required check-ins such as these might encourage members to prioritize committee-related work and to exert supportive peer pressure on the individual who is not meeting committee goals.

**Implement discussion rules.** Robert's Rules of Order have been used to manage discussions for years, but the system itself is clunky and not always well understood. Simplifying discussion rules can help a committee be more creative and engage in constructive conflict. Work with members early, perhaps even in the team charter produced during the retreat or planning meeting, to set agreed-upon guidelines for discussions, and use the timer in the way the team agreed, reminding them of their consensus as you do. Consider implementing the following suggestions:

Maintain a large sticky note or a Google Doc in which both the agenda and major discussion points are written down and prioritized immediately, allowing the committee members to see the discussion as it flows and to stay on task.

Use a timer or assign a certain number of "chips" that each member can use to contribute to the discussion. These strategies allow you to limit the amount of time spent on each agenda item or how long each person can speak on a point.

Use a "parking lot" to keep discussions on track without losing ideas or points not relevant to the discussion at hand. People will often bring up points that relate to their personal interests or good ideas that are not relevant at the time. Recognize when these points are raised or are interrupting the discussion, ask the speaker if that idea can be tabled for now, and "park" the idea on a separate sticky note or Google Doc section for review or discussion at a later date.

## Managing Conflict

One of the most important things a committee leader must do is facilitate conflict that leads to consensus. Agile and collaboration researchers universally acknowledge that constructive conflict is necessary for collaborative groups to innovate and make progress (see, for example, Adkins, 2010; Kilby, 2013; Hansen, 2009; Sawyer, 2007). Committee members, like any other group of strong-minded individuals, will disagree along the way. Common disagreements can stem from too much passion to not enough engagement, from lack of understanding of process to lack of agreement on goals, from those with personal agendas speaking over those with softer voices. Below are some facilitation techniques used by Agile coaches that can keep a discussion on track and encourage participation:

Five Whys. Discussions can often spin out of control when a group has different understandings of a problem or charge. One way to more clearly articulate a perceived problem, whether one of direct importance to the committee charge or one perceived as such, is the Five Whys strategy. Begin by asking the person raising the issue to state the problem as they see it in one sentence. As chair, ask "why?" and allow the speaker to respond. Repeat this ask and reply series four more times. This process requires the speaker to explain why the issue as they see it is relevant to the committee's charge at the time. Doing so allows the group to more clearly think through the possible roots of the perceived problem and to hopefully get to the real issue quickly so that it can be addressed or removed from consideration.

**Forced ranking.** If the committee members become divided on what stories or tasks should be prioritized at any stage and this begins to hamper progress, the forced ranking activity can "force" members to make hard decisions about next steps. Members will need a list of the stories at issue and a small number of criteria against which to judge them. Criteria might include "Most relevant to the final report," "Most likely to provide the best data," or "Most important to our understanding of the issue," for example. Each member then assigns each story a rank based on the criteria and on how many items are being ranked. If six items are in question, the committee members rank stories 1 through 6 in order using each number only once. Numbers are then tallied; stories with the lowest numbers are considered to be of highest priority to the team as a whole (Gray, Brown & Macanufo, 2010, pp. 67–68).

**Fist of Five or Roman votes.** The Fist of Five method of consensus is outlined above and can be used to check the pulse of the committee at any point during the discussion. Any member of the committee can call for this vote, just as anyone can call the question in Robert's Rules. Remember that the goal of Fist of Five is not necessarily to make sure everyone agrees, but to see where people stand at the time. A variation of Fist of Five is the Roman vote, which, like in the gladiatorial arena, uses a thumbs up, thumbs down, and thumbs sideways to illustrate a person's opinion on an issue. Roman voting can be used to take a team's pulse as well. Physical voting requires everyone to make a decision quickly, gives everyone an equal voice, and allows immediate conversation because everyone has seen the vote results.

### Department Chairs

These strategies can also be used proactively to manage department meetings, provided that department members have learned about and agreed upon discussion guidelines during a retreat or planning meeting.

Committee leaders can employ these strategies to encourage participation from all members and to guide the group subtly toward progress and consensus. Leading a committee, especially one composed of vocal and passionate faculty, can be challenging and gratifying. These strategies provide additional options for ensuring productive discussions and decision-making.

## Wrapping Up

Committee service and leadership are necessary and valuable parts of our academic careers. Committee work moves the university mission forward and allows faculty strong voices in the life of the university. Scrum provides a framework for approaching our committee work as incremental progress toward goals by managing team dynamics, discussions, and contributions to the agreed-upon charge. When committee members work together as an Agile team led by a strong servant-leader-peer, faculty can transform the way they approach work toward shared goals.

In the next chapter, we'll explore how other Agile strategies can be adapted to frame more personal, one-on-one mentoring relationships between faculty members and student advisees, undergraduate or graduate researchers, and peers.

# 6

# Mentoring Students and Peers
# with Agile Activities

After reading this chapter, you will be able to

- Draw on the Agile mindset and values to consider mentoring a team activity
- Advise students to develop high-level course-of-study
  plans using epics and stories
- Support undergraduate and graduate researchers using
  the Scrum framework
- Collegially mentor junior faculty drawing on Agile planning
  and estimating strategies
- Use Agile coaching strategies to support successful mutual
  mentoring groups

We probably all know the story of the first mentor, the friend
to whom Odysseus charged the care and education of his son
Telemachus while he was away. Athena, goddess of wisdom,
borrowed Mentor's form on several occasions to bestow knowledge on her favored. From this we get the modern definition

of a mentor as someone who supports, assists, and imparts wisdom to a less-experienced peer or student. Mentoring is a central part of our endeavors as faculty when we advise students who are majoring in our programs and conducting research, take a new faculty member or a colleague under wing, or develop a supportive relationship with fellow mid-career faculty.

We all have experienced and provided mentoring in our faculty careers; some relationships were likely more effective than others. Yet graduate school does not often prepare future faculty to create successful mentor-mentee relationships. In the team mindset of Agile and Scrum, mentoring undergirds the foundational philosophy and is a primary duty for Scrum Masters and Agile coaches. In this Scrum mindset, we assume that each person is doing the best he or she can at any given moment and that with collegial openness, courage, and respect, each person is capable of significant growth. With this mindset, Agile is an excellent foundation on which to ground mentoring activities.

Building on this perspective in this chapter, I will briefly review a few relevant ideas about mentoring and imagine what the mentor-mentee relationship might look like when built on an Agile team foundation. I will then examine how to apply Scrum practices within common mentoring relationships—student advisees, graduate and undergraduate researchers, and academic peers—in order to help mentees make the best choices for meeting personal goals. Like the previous chapter on committees, this chapter outlines a potentially new application of Agile not yet applied or studied in higher education. I hypothesize that mentor-mentee relationships can function like micro-teams and mirror the relationship between an Agile coach and a team member. The strategies in this chapter combine mentoring theory, Agile coaching approaches, and the Scrum process to suggest how Agile mentoring relationships can develop and prosper.

## Understanding Mentorship as an Agile Teaching Activity

Take a minute to think about a mentor in your professional or personal life. Which of this person's qualities do you respect most? What do you both get out of the relationship? Our mentors served as teachers, models, therapists, devil's advocates, coaches, editors, and rear-end kickers. Hopefully, as mentees, we also pushed our mentors in intellectual, scholarly, and professional ways. A good mentoring relationship is like a two-person team, though with a discernible power dynamic special to the relationship, and good teams require a solid foundation.

Mentoring and advising are core faculty activities, ones that offer mutual benefits and satisfaction. According to the authors of *Academic Advising: A Comprehensive Handbook*, the goal of advising today is to "achieve student success through teaching and learning that results in effective career and life planning" (Gordon, Habley & Grites, 2011, p. 2), certainly something we should want for all of our students.

The mentoring relationship can be one of the most profound in a person's life. W. Brad Johnson (2007) argues that "when students encounter a faculty mentor who gets to know them, refrains from rejecting them as unworthy (something many college and graduate students fully expect), and instead offers acceptance, confirmation, admiration, and emotional support, their self-concepts are irrevocably bolstered" (p. 9).

Many faculty members can point to the person who believed in them and pushed them to achieve their potential, thus helping them become the people they are today. For students and faculty alike, mentors provide "socialization, learning, career advancement, psychological adjustment, and preparation for leadership" (Johnson, 2007, p. 4). A good mentor helps a mentee scaffold personal development and adapt paths as opportunities for growth or challenges arise, thus helping the mentee to become more consciously reflective and flexible (Shore, 2014, pp. 41, 43). Our mentors are our partners, models we follow as we are initiated into a discipline, institution, and profession. In turn, we as faculty members return the favor by providing developmental support to our undergraduates, graduate students, and peers.

Mentoring is also central to the Agile mindset. Part of what the authors of the *Agile Manifesto* were reacting against was a traditional human capital view in software development that treated people as resources to be 100 percent allocated during work hours. Because humans are not robots and software development is a creative endeavor, developers in this system rarely met goals and often burned out under the stress. Agile was developed from an opposite perspective, seeing humans as learning beings who thrive under conditions that allow creativity, flexibility, autonomy, learning, and trust among peers. This is achieved through close collaboration in teams and mentoring offered between team members and by Agile coaches and Scrum Masters.

Drawing on the Scrum process and Agile coaching strategies, faculty can structure mentoring activities in a variety of relationships to help mentees address personal goals and professional development. Now we will look at some specific mentoring activities where the Scrum process might be applied when working with a mentee. First, let's examine ways to help students plan their academic careers.

## Using Epics and Stories with Undergraduate Mentees

Many faculty advise students as they create plans for their educational careers. While graduate students might have a clearer idea of what they must do to accomplish specific goals, undergraduates may have more difficulty choosing among the variety of options available to them over four years, especially when trying to develop a four-year plan for their time in college. A typical four-year plan for an undergraduate might resemble the grid in table 6.1. Students and advisors use the grid to map out courses that the students must complete and experiences they want to have (internships, undergraduate research, study abroad, etc.). For my own first-year advisees, completing the grid is either an exercise in learning to control choices or one of outright panic.

With an Agile mindset, students can reimagine an academic plan as a backlog of meaningful epics and stories. Doing so encourages under-

TABLE 6.1  Simple four-year planning rubric

|  | First-Year | Sophomore | Junior | Senior |
|---|---|---|---|---|
| Fall |  |  |  |  |
| Winter |  |  |  |  |
| Spring |  |  |  |  |
| Summer |  |  |  |  |

graduates to think beyond the scary "What do you *want to do* with your life?" to a more flexible "What do you *want to be able to do* with your life?" Course planning becomes about developing the right skill sets rather than training for a particular job, which may be reassuring to many first-year students. Like developers on a Scrum team who make decisions about what to do next only when they have the most information, helping mentees focus on life goals before a singular path can help them see more flexibility in their academic careers and make better decisions over time based on broader personal goals formulated as epics.

As discussed in chapter 2, a story is a piece of functionality that the development team can typically complete in one sprint and that allows the user to do something he or she wants to do. An epic, on the other hand, is a large, complex story that will require the team to explore, collect information, and analyze the context in detail before articulating the stories required to complete the epic. When crafting epics and stories, teams often use this language:

> As a <type of user>, I want to be able to <some goal> so that I can <some reason>.

The formula allows the team to keep the end user in mind and to define tasks they can do to help the user meet specific goals. What does this have to do with mentoring? Well, the other, more common definition of epic is "a heroic quest." Scaffolding one's education to make the most of one's life as a person, professional, and citizen is a fairly heroic enterprise. Students, like Scrum team members, must explore, collect information and experiences, and make informed choices about possible paths. Using the epic/story construct can help them focus on authentic goals for the future, the "why" over the "how," so to speak.

So rather than starting with the four-year plan grid, you might

1. **Help students articulate their epics** using the story formula modified in this way:

   > As a <student/professional/citizen>, I want to be able to <some goal> so that I can <some reason>.

Epics should be complex enough to take multiple steps to achieve, discrete enough that they can actually be accomplished, and flexible enough that there are several paths to satisfying the goals. Example student epics might include

> *As a student, I want to be able to complete an undergraduate research project in a field of my choosing so that I can determine if I want to go to graduate school or into the workforce.*

> *As a citizen, I want to be able to speak fluent Spanish so that I can work with Mexican immigrants in my community, either through my career or through service.*

> *As a future professional, I want to be able to effectively run my own small business so that I can contribute to my local economy and support other small businesses.*

Essentially, each student begins a backlog for his or her future that focuses on personal goals rather than checking off courses in a curriculum.

2. **Encourage students to prioritize their epics according to their most motivating goals.** The act of prioritizing provides a reflective opportunity to examine goals, to see what rises to the top, and to discuss why. This informed perspective can help students articulate the possible paths to reach those goals.

3. **Break down the epics into academic and co-curricular stories that might help students accomplish goals.** Stories are more discrete goals toward accomplishing an epic; the student should be able to complete associated tasks in a shorter amount of time, perhaps a few weeks or a semester. For example, using the citizenship epic above, the student might brainstorm stories like these:

> *As a student, I want to complete a major in Spanish so that I can achieve technical fluency for my service and professional life.*

> *As a student, I want to major in Latin American Studies so that I can be prepared to address issues facing the Mexican immigrant in collaboration with local leaders.*

*As a student, I want to volunteer with a Spanish-speaking
community so that I can determine if I want to pursue a
career or volunteer role with this group in the future.*

4. **Map the stories and associated tasks.** Starting with the epic
   or story the student is most interested in at the time, articulate
   discrete tasks the student can do to work toward the goal. For
   example, using the volunteering story above, the student might
   create tasks including "determine local programs supporting
   Mexican immigrants," "determine personal criteria for type of
   program to work with," "meet with directors of each program,"
   "observe volunteers in action," "choose an organization," and
   "begin to volunteer." You might use a grid like table 6.1 to map
   out these different possibilities, such as the different paths
   articulated in the student's two possible major stories. Or the
   student might find a mind mapping activity valuable. A mind
   map is a free association brainstorming tool that allows the person to visually articulate possibilities and their relationships to
   each other. Mind maps can be drawn on a big piece of paper or
   created using available software, such as the sample in figure 6.1.

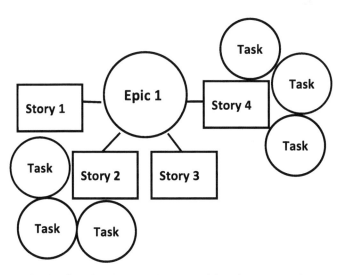

**Fig. 6.1** Sample mind map planning tool for a first-year student

Visualizing the possible paths via chart or mind map helps the student see different options more clearly.

5. **Use the epics and stories in each advising session.** Epics and stories are flexible and can be added or removed as students develop clearer pictures of their future selves. These articulations, rather than the four-year-plan grid, are where the mentoring can happen. A student's backlog that is groomed each semester can be used as the foundation of the advising meeting to reassess goals and make decisions using the most current information about interests and experiences.

While I have focused on undergraduates, the Agile mentoring process described above can also be used with graduate students. Because faculty who advise graduate students are often research mentors as well, the next section covers how to use the broader Scrum framework as a tool to mentor graduate and undergraduate students through the research and professionalization process.

## Mentoring Research Students

Working with both undergraduate and graduate student researchers is often a highlight of faculty work. Mentoring is first and foremost a teaching activity, and while undergraduates may be less likely to become professional researchers than graduate students, mentoring at both levels requires discipline-specific experience and attention to how the research experience translates into transferable skills. The Scrum cycle (see chapter 2) provides a logical order to the often-messy research process, helps students realize incremental progress, creates an environment for learning from mistakes, and fosters active reflection on personal and professional growth.

As discussed in chapters 3 and 4, the Scrum sprinting cycle translates well to research projects large and small. When mentoring research students, the faculty mentor role becomes that of a facilitator and resource as the students do their research under your guidance. Consider the following activities to successfully begin a research mentoring relationship:

1. **Build your team foundation.** According to Brad Johnson (2007), the mentor and mentee should "design" the mentoring relationship early, including examining each person's expectations of the other, making sure mutual goals are clear, establishing guidelines (and boundaries) for interactions, articulating time commitments, and addressing any additional concerns (pp. 85–88). To design the relationship effectively, create a mentoring charter, a set of mutually defined ground rules, shared values, and expectations regarding how to interact, communicate, and work with each other to achieve your mutual goals. Doing so will ground a supportive mentoring environment and provide a touchstone throughout the relationship.

## Sample Charter for Mentoring Activities of Jane Hayes (mentee) and Valerie Burke (mentor)

*Meetings:* First Tuesday of every month during Fall semester, 3pm at Coffee House

*Communication:* Emails to exchange information, will respond within 48 hours to simple questions. If a larger question arises, a short discussion will be scheduled within three days whenever possible.

*Time Commitments:* We agree that we will devote at least 6 hours in conversation over the course of the fall semester. Jane agrees to create her initial backlog before the first meeting and share it with Dr. Burke at least three days before the first meeting. Dr. Burke agrees to read and keep up with Jane's backlog over the course of the semester.

*Goals:* To leverage Dr. Burke's publication experience to support Jane as she shops her book proposal to academic publishers and as she continues to revise her dissertation into a publishable manuscript. To help Jane develop her own acceptable balance between research, teaching, service, and personal well-being. To introduce Dr. Burke to ethnography as a research method in the field using Jane's dissertation/manuscript as a case study.

2. **Create and prioritize the backlog.** This can be the most intimidating part of the process for students new to research because there are so many unknowns. While a product owner in an Agile organization is in charge of maintaining the backlog for a team, mentors work in concert with mentees to develop the initial backlog, especially if a student is designing his or her own project rather than joining a project already in progress. By listing the epics for the research, you help students see the forest without overwhelming them with the trees. Next, help students prioritize the epics and develop stories for the top priorities.

3. **Plan the first sprint.** Many Scrum teams starting a new project will start their work with "sprint 0," during which they collect information they need to start the first official sprint. They might need to become familiar with new software or equipment, learn more about users or how the project fits into the overall business, etc. Sprint 0 for a research student might include a preliminary review of relevant literature, learning a specific lab procedure, or reading up on the research method he or she will be using. If the student is already prepared to get started, take the stories you think can reasonably be completed in a defined sprint interval and help the student plot the associated tasks.

4. **Visualize the work.** Physical Scrum boards allow teams to move sticky notes representing stories and tasks across the Backlog, Work in Progress (WIP), and Done columns (see chapter 2), which has been known to cause a valuable psychological boost in teams. But blank boards or walls can often be a luxury in academic research spaces. Shared Google Docs and free academic versions of Agile software, including those by Version-One, LeanKit, and Basecamp, can be used if physical space is at a premium. Help the student transfer the stories and tasks for the first sprint onto the board or into the tool and move the first tasks into the WIP column to kick off the sprint.

5. **Have Scrum commitment meetings during the sprint.** While faculty outside of lab settings may not work with research students every day, daily or weekly Scrum meetings can be used to discuss process, progress, questions, and impediments to the

research (see chapter 2). Consider using mentoring meetings to update the Scrum board and to coach student researchers. You might share useful resources, help a student think through a mental block, boost confidence through formative feedback, or assist in developing an approach to challenges or unexpected obstacles.

6. **Hold review and retrospective meetings.** At the end of a sprint, have a longer meeting with the research student to review the work accomplished and discuss his or her process. Ask the student to provide a progress report or other deliverable that presents the work so far before you meet. In the review part of the meeting, the student can formally or informally present the work accomplished during the sprint. Use the time to support and challenge the student as necessary. In addition to the review, use part of the time for a retrospective to discuss the research sprint process, what the student is learning or needs to look into more, and how to jointly improve your interactions for the next sprint.

At the end of each research sprint, begin the cycle again with a planning meeting. By keeping true to the sprint cycle, mentor and mentee establish a rhythm for the project that supports planning, executing tasks, showing incremental progress, and reflecting on learning. Sprinting requires progress, even if that means adapting to new information, disappointing results, or big changes. By coaching students through the project and the sprinting process, faculty as mentors help students manage work but also learn how to deal with the unknowns and messiness of research, skills that can transfer into any field or workplace.

### Department Chairs

Consider sharing this mentoring system with your faculty in a workshop. It may give them a push to reconsider their mentoring approach and their own goals for mentoring activities.

The practices discussed in the previous sections can be adapted to any mentoring relationship. The remainder of this chapter offers advice for adapting these strategies, with a few new tricks, to mentor other faculty members. The first section that follows addresses mentoring of new faculty, and the second section discusses how these strategies can be adopted by mutual mentoring groups.

## Mentoring New Faculty

Faculty work has a unique cadence, and supporting new and junior faculty in their professional growth has long been the subject of research in higher education (see, for example, Boice, 1992; Eisenhardt et al., 2008; Foote & Solem, 2009; Mamiseishvil, 2012; Yun & Sorcinelli, 2009). Career planning can be especially complex for new faculty who have many choices about how to teach, what research path to follow, and how to serve the institution, the discipline, and the community. When more senior faculty mentor new faculty, a natural power relationship exists, but as Jeffrey L. Buller (2012), author of *The Essential Department Chair*, notes, our role in mentoring faculty "is similar to what you do when advising students: you don't want to dictate every aspect of what the person does or experiences, but you can provide sound guidance that can help the person in making some appropriate choices" (p. 283). As when advising students, mentors can help new faculty mentees work through career goals using epics and stories and a visualized but adaptable plan of action.

### New Faculty

Seek out mentors in your program, department, and institution early. Peers, chairs, deans, and directors of teaching and learning centers can be good resources when you are looking for mentors because they are likely to be more familiar with faculty who might be a good match. If you think the Scrum mentoring system would work for you, introduce it to them in an initial meeting, and open the discussion.

Below are some suggested steps for mentoring new faculty members the Agile way, grounded in the earlier advice in this chapter:

1.  **Create a mentoring team charter to set guidelines for the working relationship.** The best mentoring relationships are grounded on similar expectations, as discussed above. Understanding each other's time constraints, preferred means of contact, a mutually agreed upon number of meetings, and specific topics for the relationship can lay a valuable foundation. For example, a mentoring pair might decide to meet every second Wednesday of the semester for lunch and to hold planning and review meetings at the beginning and end of a semester. They might then decide that the main topics for the semester will be helping the new faculty member achieve a balance between research, teaching, and service goals as well as work-life balance.

2.  **Help mentees articulate the epics of their professional work for a given time period using a modified story format:**

    *As a <professional, instructor, researcher, or citizen> of the <department, institution, discipline, and/or community>, I want to be able to <do something specific> so that I can <meet some goal>.*

    Explain the rationale behind articulating goals as epics, and share a few of your own epics as models. Encourage the mentee to consider specific goals for one, five, and ten years from now or until the next major achievement, such as securing tenure or publishing a book. Having long-term goals can make prioritizing immediate goals in the next step easier. For example, a new faculty member might generate epics such as the following:

    *As a new instructor, I want to develop an effective pedagogical strategy in my introductory course so that I can prepare students to meet the goals of the program.*

    *As a new academic, I want to publish a book from my dissertation so that I can establish a record as an active scholar in my discipline.*

*As a new community member, I want to partner with one local organization so that I can be a good citizen and build a relationship for future course opportunities.*

3. **Help your mentee prioritize epics.** According to willpower researchers Baumeister and Tierney (2011), for many people, "the problem is not a lack of goals but rather too many of them" (p. 63). As someone who has been through the process already, you can help the mentee prioritize the goals that most likely lead to success at this point in his or her the academic career. If at a research-intensive university, you might help the mentee prioritize the book; however, at a teaching-intensive institution, you might encourage the mentee to find a balance between teaching, research, and service.

4. **Break down the epics into stories** that might help the mentee accomplish these goals. What are small but achievable steps that the mentee can make toward that goal, including necessary learning required before steps can be taken? For example, using the book epic above, the mentee might start with these stories:

*As an author, I want to work with my mentor to create a revision plan for my dissertation so that I can make it more publishable.*

*As an author, I want to choose the appropriate publisher for my manuscript submission so that I can increase the chance of publication.*

*As an author, I want to write a book proposal that will impress my chosen publisher and earn a contract for publication.*

*As an author, I want to update my literature review chapter to ensure it is current and valuable to the reader.*

Then help the mentee break the stories into tasks. For the book proposal story, tasks might include "research appropriate publishers," "download and read proposal guidelines," "research competing texts," "articulate readership for book," etc.

5. **Estimate and prioritize the backlog.** Successfully estimating and prioritizing career backlog items can help faculty at all career stages make better decisions about how and on what to spend time. T-shirt sizing is one strategy that can be used to visualize the complexity of different career backlog items, which may aid with prioritizing. Using this strategy, each story is assigned a "T-shirt size" ranging from XS for extra small stories that can be completed quickly to XL or XXL stories that are extra or extra-extra large and will take potentially years to accomplish. The career backlog in step 2 above lists three epics of different sizes. The mentor and mentee working on this career backlog might assign these three epics different T-shirt sizes (see fig. 6.2; see chapter 4 for additional advice).

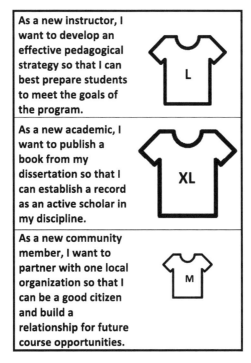

**Fig. 6.2** Using T-shirt sizing to estimate and prioritize career stories

With this visualization, the mentor and mentee have another tool to use to prioritize. Because developing a partner relationship is the smallest of the epics, that might be one the mentee can accomplish in one semester by investigating different organizations and volunteering with one. For the other, larger and more complex epics, the pair can now have a discussion about which component stories can be successfully completed given the time constraints in a semester.

6. **Create a sprint backlog for a chosen amount of time based on priorities.** For a new faculty member just getting used to the rhythms of faculty life, sprints of one month may be appropriate, while for junior faculty with a few years behind them, a one-semester sprint might be effective as long as the mentee (and the mentor if meeting throughout the semester) update the backlog and board regularly. Use the prioritized career backlog (which represents the mentee's goals), the mentee's understanding of his or her own work habits, and your experience as a more senior faculty with what can realistically be accomplished in the sprint time frame to create the sprint plan with the mentee.

7. **Map the stories for the sprint visually, and explore how the mentee can use a Scrum board to track progress.** Encourage the mentee to create a physical board in an office or lab space to promote sustained focus on the goals at hand. In my office, I have two boards. One is a large sticky note on the back of my door that lists my one-, five-, and ten-year epics. I see them every time I hang up or retrieve my coat. Second, I have a sprint board, usually from a monthly or semester section of my backlog, on which I visualize my current epics broken down into stories and tasks. I tend to use this board for my research activities only, but a mentee might find it useful to maintain one for any aspect of a career backlog. Consider modeling Agile career planning by sharing your Scrum boards with your mentee if you use them.

8. **Review epics and stories regularly with the mentee, perhaps at the beginning and end of a semester.** The career-planning backlog is meant to be adaptable so that the mentee can adjust it as new opportunities and challenges present themselves. Just as

you would begin any Scrum cycle with sprint planning and end with a review and retrospective, use the career-planning backlog to help the mentee prioritize a few epics or stories for a semester and to review progress. While looking at the backlog, talk with the mentee about what can realistically be accomplished in a semester, set goals, and then, at the end of the semester, review what was accomplished. Use this opportunity to revise goals and to continue planning for the next semester or year.

This Agile mentored career-planning process can help set the tone for a productive first few years for the mentee new to your university context and set the tone for dynamic mentoring discussions.

One rule most Scrum teams have is to not change work during the sprint unless it absolutely cannot be avoided. This allows the team to commit and focus on the work at hand, holding potential changes for the next grooming and planning sessions. Using this philosophy, encourage the mentee to keep track of new possibilities and challenges in the career-planning backlog but to stay the course on priorities identified for the month or semester, unless the opportunity is fleeting or the challenge is a true impediment.

While much has been written on orienting and helping new faculty succeed in academia, research in the last ten years has turned to a much larger group of faculty who can also benefit from collegial mentoring— mid-career faculty.

## Mutual Faculty Mentoring

Mid- and late career faculty face challenges that are much different than those faced by new faculty. Research has shown that once faculty achieve promotion and tenure, they enter a time of increased service expectations, and new opportunities for leadership and self-direction, but it is also potentially a time of feeling adrift, unnoticed, and unmotivated while contemplating the next 20 to 30 years of their careers (see, for example, Baldwin & Chang, 2006; Baldwin et al., 2008; Baldwin, Lunceford, & Vanderlinden, 2005; Canale, Herdklotz, & Wild, 2013; Stange & Merdinger, 2014).

When faculty hit mid-career, being a "protégé" in the traditional mentor-mentee hierarchical relationship can be less attractive, while collegial support, resources for success, and reinforcement of value to the institution become more important (Baldwin & Chang, 2006). Mutual mentoring and networked mentoring efforts are becoming more popular among mid-career faculty and the centers that support their continued development. In a mutual mentoring relationship, a pair or group of faculty commit to supporting each other in whatever area they choose to focus on as a group, perhaps writing and research, leadership growth, work-life balance, or some combination of the like (see, for example, Fox, 2012; Pastore, 2013; Socinelli & Yun, 2007). Mutual mentoring might be similar to Etienne Wenger's (1998) concept of communities of practice as well, informal but goal-driven supportive communities of peers focused on working to address a shared concern.

Because Agile is also peer driven, learning centered, and supportive of professional development within the work context, it translates well to mutual peer mentoring among faculty. Because these relationships can often be less formal than a traditional one-on-one mentoring relationship, the strategies discussed above may be useful to help each participant develop a plan at the beginning of the group but may be too formalized for a continued relationship. Below are some ideas borrowed from Agile, Scrum, and Agile coaches that can be applied by mutual mentoring groups in addition to the team charter and backlog development strategies discussed above.

Trust and accountability with the group are arguably the most important features of a mutual mentoring group. Exercises used by Agile coaches to build trust among Scrum team members can be used by groups to lay a strong foundation for collaboration. My personal favorite is the journey line. In a journey line (Adkins, 2010) activity, the members of the mentoring group

1. silently draw line graphs representing the highs and lows of their professional journeys, adding notes about the events at the peaks and valleys (see figure 6.3);

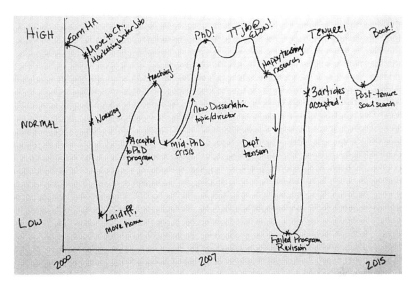

**Fig. 6.3** Sample journey line

2. take a few minutes each to talk through their journeys, using the line graphs as illustrations;
3. offer reflection observations to each other about skills, strengths, and values evident in the journey line; and
4. discuss similarities and differences in their journeys and opportunities for mutual learning during the mentoring relationship.

This exercise helps to "humanize" each person and sets the tone for a trusting and respectful experience among peers.

Another potentially useful kick-off activity can be a variation of the 4Cs strategy (Gray, Brown & Macanufo, 2010, pp. 138–140). You will need a large whiteboard, dry erase markers, sticky notes, and pens for this activity. On the white board, draw a two-by-two grid, labeling the four quadrants as "components," "characteristics," "challenges," and "characters." As a group, identify a challenge to explore such as "work-life balance as a mid-career faculty" or "being 'productive' at mid-career." Team members then individually brainstorm ideas about the topic within each of the four squares, using the following guidelines:

**Components** are smaller pieces of the topic.

**Characteristics** are attributes or traits related to the topic.

**Challenges** are barriers or impediments associated with the topic.

**Characters** are the people related to the topic or who can have impact on the topic.

Using the topic "being 'productive' at mid-career," the group might generate a grid that starts to look like the example in table 6.2.

The grid then becomes a starting point for a discussion about the topic and may help the group narrow down a focus to explore together or individually. The 4Cs activity can be used to start off a group or to encourage discussion of any new topic during a group meeting.

In addition to engendering trust, mutual mentoring groups can hold members accountable to the commitments they make to their personal goals. Patterning group meetings on the standard Scrum team meetings can build that expectation of accountability into the group's mentoring process:

**Planning.** Before or early in the semester, members identify major goals for the semester from their career backlogs. Working with

TABLE 6.2  Sample 4Cs grid for the topic "being 'productive' at mid-career"

| Components | Characteristics |
|---|---|
| Research | Lack of direct support |
| Teaching | More freedom of choice |
| Community service | Expected to self-direct |
| Disciplinary service | More service leadership |
| Institutional service | Many possible opportunities |
| | Motivation (or lack thereof) |

| Challenges | Characters |
|---|---|
| What defines "productivity"? | Faculty/us |
| Priorities at this point | Chairs |
| New goals? | Deans |
| Family (child care, elder care, relationships, etc.) | Peers also in mid-career |
| | Possibly students |
| | Faculty developers |
| | Faculty research committee |

the input of the group, members determine what they will commit to accomplishing this semester and by the next meeting so that the intention is verbalized and public.

**Daily Scrum.** At the start of each meeting, members answer the three Scrum questions: What have I accomplished toward my goals since we last met? What am I currently working on to advance my goals? and What challenges or impediments are hindering my progress? Each member makes notes about the progress of peers but gives no feedback at this time. This allows each member to report out to the group honestly about their progress and concerns.

**Review.** Performed every meeting or at the end of the semester, depending on the group's preference, reviews allow members to showcase work they have completed toward their articulated goals over a period of time. Members might bring a piece of an article, a grant proposal, proof of work with a community partner, or a revised syllabus, for example, to share with the group. The type and regularity of feedback the group provides would depend on the group's charter. Sharing actual documents or experiences for feedback encourages all of the Agile values within the group: focus, courage, commitment, openness, and respect.

**Retrospective.** Like all teams, mutual mentoring groups can benefit from an occasional check-in to ensure members still support the goals of the group and are happy with progress so far. A retrospective at the end of a semester, for example, allows the group to review its process over the course of the semester, determine areas of excellence and concern, and decide on any changes in the process or goals for the group as it continues. If the group has finished its time together, a retrospective can be a valuable capstone experience and help the team articulate any advice they might have for future groups.

Research on mutual faculty mentoring shows that many mid-career groups tend to be less formalized in terms of process than traditional one-on-one mentoring relationships. Adding several elements of Agile and Scrum can give a group a lightweight framework around which to organize activities and maximize the value of the mutual mentoring experience.

## Wrapping Up

Good faculty-citizens in higher education can thrive when providing and accepting strong mentorship. Adding an Agile perspective to these mentoring activities creates opportunities to strengthen the Agile values of focus, courage, openness, commitment, and respect and to increase satisfaction in the work faculty do in the pursuit of professional development and continuous improvement.

Building on the idea that mentor and mentee can be a team and work together to develop a plan for success, the next chapter will examine how to use goals stated as epics and stories to plan a successful course.

# 7

# Organizing Your Course as an Epic

After reading this chapter, you will be able to

- Use Agile to think about a course as an epic in the larger project of your program's curriculum
- Apply Agile concepts and backward design to develop course stories, assessment criteria, and schedules
- Consider how these practices can be used to design a new course, revise an existing course, think through a shared syllabus in a group, and conduct curriculum design or realignment

Epic—a large, complex story that will require the team to explore, collect information, and analyze the context in detail before articulating the smaller, dependent stories required to achieve the larger goal; a heroic quest.

When it comes time to revise a syllabus for a signature course or to create a new, shared syllabus for a multi-section introductory course, how do you approach that activity? For many faculty who do not have degrees in education or instructional design, creating a course plan is probably a learned skill. As a new faculty member who had never taught students in a major before, I created my first syllabi by borrowing and adapting those of my peers in the program. I added some of my own ideas about readings and content, primarily drawing from graduate seminars I had taken. Syllabi as pastiche. It took several years of trial and error before I found an effective balance of readings, activities, assignments, and projects that achieved my changing learning objectives in the courses I teach most regularly.

Designing an effective course is contingent on a vast array of dependent variables. Courses come in all shapes and sizes, from large lecture classes to intimate seminars, introductory classes with 50 sections running simultaneously to one section of an experimental course, from traditional lecture to flipped classrooms to online courses. All fit into the broader picture of the university curriculum and are intended to help students achieve specific learning goals on their paths to a degree.

In Scrum terms, epics, as defined in the chapter opening, are large stories composed of a set of smaller, dependent stories that will most likely take several sprints to complete. Epics do not produce value for the end user until all of the dependent stories have been completed. Because Scrum is a framework for work rather than a meticulous plan, teams are empowered to deconstruct the epic into realistic stories they can accomplish over time, using the built-in plan-execute-reflect learning loop of the iteration cycle to adjust their focus as necessary to be successful. Epics, then, are a perfect metaphor for individual courses within the larger project of a curriculum.

This chapter explores how faculty might use the concept of an epic to design or redesign a course by articulating it as an epic composed of learning stories, complete with associated learning outcomes—or acceptance criteria, to use an Agile software development term. I find that using a combination of backward design and an epic-story framework invigorates my course design because it allows me to articulate course goals differently and, therefore, think innovatively about my course. The first part of the chapter reviews backward design and aligns course planning with aspects of Scrum. The following sections illustrate how I have used this process to design a new course and redesign an existing course, respectively. A final section discusses how to further adapt the process for creating or redesigning a shared course syllabus and aligning an overarching curriculum. While the process I outline and illustrate is extensive, aspects of the process can easily be pulled out and used productively without following every step discussed here.

## Rethinking Backward Design as Agile Course Design

Agile project development and course design in higher education share distinct parallels, as illustrated in table 7.1. For each software application developed using Scrum, business analysts and product owners (POs) determine, based on customer feedback and competitor research, what major features could be built to address specific customer needs or desires. Within the project of the overarching application development, they create epics, which are distributed to teams. The different teams each work with a PO to articulate the component stories required to complete the epic and to create acceptance criteria for each

**TABLE 7.1**  Aligning Scrum with curriculum and course building

| Agile term | Curriculum aspect |
| --- | --- |
| Project | The overarching program curriculum |
| Epic | An individual course or experience within a curriculum |
| Story | A student learning goal or outcome for a course |
| Sprint | A time-delimited learning unit within a course during which students work to complete learning goals |
| Acceptance criteria | Assessment criteria that prove a student has achieved the learning outcomes |
| Review | Deliverable used to assess whether or not a student has accomplished the learning outcomes of the course |
| Retrospective | Formal or informal reflection on learning and process completed by a student and/or a faculty member |

story, conditions that must be met before the story can officially be called "done." Teams then work in sprints to achieve their goals for the sprint, epic, and larger project.

This process is similar to a backward design approach to course development. The two most commonly referenced structures for backward design come from L. Dee Fink's "significant learning" approach (2003) and Wiggins and McTighe's Understanding by Design (UbD) framework (2005).[1] Within both of these approaches, the process of planning a course includes

1. articulating desired outcomes for student learning within the given context of the discipline, program, and student population;
2. deciding what evidence must be collected to determine if those results have been achieved; and
3. planning the course readings, activities, and assignments to achieve these outcomes and show evidence of success.

According to Wiggins (2005), UbD "reflects a 'continuous improvement' approach to design and learning," which is exactly the Scrum mindset as illustrated in the plan-execute-reflect process (p. 14). Backward design also encourages a course structure that allows time for regular feedback, self-assessment, and reflection on learning after each unit to inform the next steps, all integral parts of the Scrum sprinting model.

Backward design and the Agile mindset combine well to help course designers achieve what collaboration researcher Keith Sawyer (2007) calls the ability to "manage a subtle balance of planning, structure, and improvisation" (p. 29). Thinking about a course as an epic breaks the learning down into stories and sprints that will help students achieve valuable learning outcomes consistently and incrementally via this combination of planning, structure, and improv. Agile faculty can use this combination of backward design and Agile thinking to begin the course development (or redesign) process with engaged student learn-

1. While the full texts of these books are available, many presentations of the approaches, both by the authors and compiled by university centers for teaching and learning, are easily accessible online. I'll use the online sources as references in the following sections so that you can pull them up and follow along as you like.

ing in mind. The next sections convey the general process for articulating a course as an epic.

## Brainstorming about the Course

Product owners and Scrum teams must carefully balance the desire to create value through innovation with what the user wants to accomplish. Similarly, faculty using Agile backward design must determine the balance between what the course must accomplish as a component in a curriculum and what the students need or want to learn for their future work, academically or professionally. I find that articulating my course's role in the curriculum and the course's learning goals in multiple ways helps me to understand the course better from many angles.

To articulate a course as an epic and possible stories associated with learning outcomes, consider addressing the questions posed in table 7.2. The questions in the left column are commonly used by Agile teams to ensure they understand the perspective of the user when considering how to develop valuable software functionality. The center column lists questions recommended by backward design proponents that can be used to ground a course goal brainstorming process. The right column presents a list of questions that I use to generate content for the epics and stories that might articulate the course.

Responding thoughtfully to several of the backward design questions generates a useful list of possibilities that can drive the overarching epic for the course and be a source of content, assignment, and assessment ideas for the rest of the design process. Once you have responded to the questions that resonate most with you, compare that list of ideas to the program goals, course description, and any personal goals you have for the course. Highlight the items on the list that fit best within those guidelines and begin to formalize the course epic and its associated stories.

## Articulating Epics and Stories

As discussed in previous chapters, software developers use a specific format to create user stories that help them keep the user's needs at

**TABLE 7.2**  Epic/story generating questions

| Questions to generate software user stories | Questions to generate learning goals using backward design | Questions to articulate course epics and stories |
|---|---|---|
| What does the user need to be able to do to achieve X goal? | What would I like the impact of this course to be on my students two to three years after the course is over? | In what context might students want to use what they will learn in the course? |
| In what context will the user be using the software when attempting to achieve X goal? | What would distinguish students who have taken this course from students who have not? | What do students already know/do that the course can build on? |
| What features is the user familiar with that we can model to help them achieve the new goal? | What essential questions will students explore? | At the end of the course, what will students be able to do that they cannot do now? |
| What hacks of existing features is the user using to achieve the desired goal with the existing functionality? | What knowledge and skills will students acquire? | At the end of the course, what will students now know that can inform their perspective on X? |
| | What meanings should students make? | At the end of the course, what additional skills will student be able to transfer to new contexts? |
| | What long-term transfer goals are targeted? | |

*Sources:* Fink, 2003, p. 8; McTighe, 2011, p. 1.

the forefront when creating a piece of functionality. This format can be adapted by faculty to articulate both an overarching statement that summarizes the course and student "user stories" that must be completed to achieve the course epic:

Software story—*As a <type of user>, I want/need to be able to <some goal or action> so that I can <accomplish some goal>.*
Course development epic—*As the <role in curriculum>, this course serves to <purpose of course> so that students will <know and/or do something>.*

Student-centered course story—*As a <type of student>, I want to be able to <know/do something> so that I can <accomplish some goal> after completing this course.*

Using the epic format requires one to think deeply about the overarching concern of a course in relation to both students and program curriculum while also being concise. The format can generate an equivalent of an elevator speech for the course:

*As the gateway research methods course to the senior capstone, this course serves to teach history majors how to conduct archival research so that they might successfully complete their own research for required thesis projects.*

*As the multi-section introductory course for biology majors and an optional general studies course for non-majors, this course serves to introduce students to foundational biological terms, concepts, and empirical techniques so that they can better understand the biological world around them and be prepared for future study.*

Drawing from the list created in the previous step, draft a few possible epic statements that might encapsulate the course and its goals. Revise and iterate until you are happy with one specific epic. Then, using your initial brainstormed list and any previously articulated course goals you might have on file, generate as many student-centered stories as possible. You might start by reviewing the brainstorm to identify recurrent themes, for example. Resist censoring yourself initially; instead, see what you can generate. Once you have a pool of stories, you can begin to align them with the course epic, course description, and curriculum the course serves.

Choose the stories that accomplish the goals of the course and that can be completed in the time allotted for the course (semester, quarter, etc.). Additionally, make sure stories are "Goldilocks tasks," which are "challenges that are not too hot or too cold, neither overly difficult nor overly simple" (Pink, 2009, p. 116). Revise stories that are too simple or too complex to make them challenging but achievable for students. For example, the course epic

*As the gateway research methods course to the senior capstone, this course serves to teach history majors how to conduct archival research so that they might successfully complete their own research for required thesis projects*

might break down into stories like these:

*As a third-year history major, I want to be able to articulate a good research question so that I can do my own senior research.*

*As a third-year history major, I want to understand different methods of conducting historical research so that I can choose the best method to address my senior research question.*

*As a third-year history major, I want to be able to collect and analyze data so that I can develop a reasonable answer to my research question.*

Once you have developed a solid list, prioritize the stories into a clear learning backlog for the course as an epic. How you prioritize is up to you—it might be from foundational to complex concepts, by steps in a specific process (as illustrated in the history example), or by most important to "bonus" stories. From here, create assessment criteria for the epic and each story.

## Determining Assessment Criteria for Epics

Backward design proponents argue that the ultimate goal of our courses should be for students to be able to both understand and transfer learning into new contexts (Wiggins, 2005, p. 14). As such, course assessment criteria should be based on what we want our students to *know* and be able to *do* at the end of the course, which exactly parallels a Scrum team's desire to create functionality that allows a user to *do* something with the software.

When building a sprint backlog, Scrum team members work with the PO not only to carefully articulate each story but also to determine "acceptance criteria" for each story, defined above as conditions that must be met before the story can be called done. For the sample epic *As a savvy entrepreneur using social media to promote my small business, I want to be able to add text to any product image I want to post so that I don't have to switch applications to add a text layer to the images*, acceptance criteria might include

> User can open photo editor within primary application.
> User can choose to add text to image.
> User can select from multiple typefaces and weights.
> User can edit text already added to image.

Acceptance criteria for a course development epic are essentially assessment criteria, ways we can evaluate whether students have met the course objectives and completed the stories of the course successfully. Assessment criteria for the history course epic above might include

> Student can articulate a viable archival research question.
> Student can select appropriate archival research methods to address a research question.
> Student can collect useful data using a selected research method.
> Student can use an appropriate data coding process to analyze data within context of a research question.
> Student can present findings in a well-written report using Chicago style.

Similarly, assessment criteria can be broken out by story as well. For the first story in the list above, assessment criteria might include

> Student can articulate a clear area of interest for a possible study.
> Student can review appropriate literature to determine a potential gap to be filled with research.
> Student can explain the gap in the existing literature clearly.
> Student can create a narrow and valid research question to address that gap in the literature.

Framing assessment criteria in this way can inform decisions about both course and assignment design.

To articulate assessment criteria using this Scrum acceptance criteria model, consider the following steps:

1.  **Begin with the highest priority story in your course backlog from the previous section, and list ways a student can prove he or she has completed that story.** Good Scrum acceptance criteria are yes/no values—the user either can or cannot successfully do something. While learning is not this black and white, yes/no criteria are a place to start when thinking about student learning and potential assignments to assess that learning.

2.  **Follow this process for all the stories in your course backlog until you have several assessment criteria for each story.**

3.  **Review for incomplete or ambiguous criteria.** Try to be specific and think of how you would actually assess for the criteria. For example, "Demonstrate critical thinking skills about X" is difficult to assess for, so how can you be specific about which critical thinking skills you want students to demonstrate in that story?

4.  **Review your stories one more time, confirming that your stories are useful and that the criteria for each can be achieved, keeping the idea of "Goldilocks tasks" in mind.** If a story has only one evaluation criterion, consider how it might be integrated into another existing story. If a story has too many criteria, it might be too complex and need to be broken into smaller stories with a reasonable number of assessment criteria. The process might also reveal that the course is trying to accomplish too much, which might lead you to reexamine priorities for the course and possibly the course's place in the curriculum.

Another valuable way to evaluate your assessment criteria is to cross-check them with a model such as Bloom's taxonomy or Wiggins and McTighe's six facets of learning. For example, you might create a chart similar to the one in table 7.3 to ensure you are touching on each of the facets of learning that you must in the course.

This extensive preplanning is another way to approach course de-

TABLE 7.3 Sample heuristic for determining learning assessment criteria

| Story | Explain | Interpret | Apply | Empathize | Illustrate perspective | Self-assess |
|---|---|---|---|---|---|---|
| Story 1 | x | x | | | | |
| Story 2 | | | x | x | | |
| Story 3 | | x | | | x | |
| Etc. | | | | x | | x |

velopment that can be used independently or in conjunction with tra-ditional methods faculty might use to create or revise courses. I appreciate this combination of backward design and Agile because it helps me to think about my course on multiple levels and design the course plan based on this deep understanding.

## Framing the Course Schedule

In software development, one of the major Scrum innovations was to move away from extensive initial project planning to a more flexible plan-emergent strategy. After completing this invention process, a course schedule will likely have started to coalesce in your mind. Considering this pre-work, logically plan a course in sprints with associated learning stories. Each sprint should be self-contained, but its successful completion should be necessary for the next sprint. Plan learning activities, outline readings, and develop assignments for both formative and summative assessment.

To develop the preliminary plan for the course as an epic, draw on previously created student stories and acceptance criteria to map sprints and learning activities using the following steps:

1. **Starting with the prioritized backlog of student stories, break up the stories you want to address together into a series of sprints.**
2. **Estimate how much time students will need to fulfill the**

assessment criteria for each story, and map the stories onto the course calendar, adjusting as necessary. Consider starting off the course with a short sprint 0 to set the tone for the course and introduce students to the processes, learning goals, and any basic content they need to succeed before jumping into the work.

3. **Determine resources needed to successfully meet each sprint's assessment criteria, and map those onto the sprints as well.** Resources might include primary and optional readings, tutorials, videos or other media, discussion topics, study guides, etc.

4. **Outline the activities that will guide students through each sprint, thinking in terms of both daily activities and specific assignments.** Depending on the course, an assignment for each sprint might be effective, and activities can work toward those end-of-sprint assignments. On the other hand, assignments that build on previous sprint products and end in one culminating project can be equally as valuable as students see how ongoing work contributes to larger goals for learning.

5. **Loosely frame the daily or weekly course plan for each sprint.** Agile and Scrum approaches assume that heavy up-front planning can be problematic down the road when unexpected challenges or opportunities arise and subvert a tight schedule. Keeping the course plan loosely structured gives students the opportunity to help shape some of the work they will do in each sprint while keeping you attuned to what the students need at any given moment.

6. **Consider using the Scrum meetings to frame sprints.** How might inviting students to help plan some of the learning in the sprint be valuable? Might a variation of daily Scrum meetings at the beginning of certain classes allow students to check their learning or coordinate with team members? How might a deliverable review at the end of a sprint demonstrate learning? Might a learning retrospective for individual students or teams elucidate how students can best learn in the next sprint? Think about

ways in which these types of activities can reinforce student learning, and implement one or all of the strategies if useful.

7. **Review and finalize the course framework, leaving time for exploration, failure, pivots, and unanticipated opportunities.** Agile leaders make decisions about the project at the *last responsible moment* since that is when they have the most information about their immediate circumstances. Keeping the course plan structured according to your stories and learning goals but loose enough to partner with students at each stage allows you to adjust on the fly.

Remember when developing an Agile course framework to strive for that balance of "planning, structure, and improvisation" that gives students power over their learning within a flexible framework to organize efforts (Sawyer, 2007, p. 29). When creating these plans, think of yourself as the product owner for the course in charge of setting up and prioritizing the backlog of student stories needed to achieve the course learning goals. A tighter calendar is useful for courses that must cover a good deal of content or parallel other sections of the course running simultaneously. A looser calendar works well for more advanced courses, especially in a major, when students have more background knowledge to draw on to design their learning within the course sprints. Create the schedule that works best for students and the contextual variables acting on the course.

To illustrate this Agile backward design process, I will next walk through the process I used to, first, design a new grant-writing course and, second, to redesign my existing 300-level publishing course. I offer my courses here as examples rather than models. While my courses tend to be small and hands-on, the model can be scaled to other types of courses including multi-section courses, large lecture courses, online courses, etc. The final section in this chapter will describe possible ways to extend this process to different types of courses.

### Faculty and Program Directors

While my courses are small and writing intensive, the same process discussed above can be used for a variety of different types of courses. For example, using the invention process might help you identify places in large lecture sections where teaching assistants can run smaller breakout discussions or team projects that meet the overall course goals. The process is transferable and scalable because it is primarily an invention strategy that can be used to help better articulate course goals and learning using epics, stories, and assessment criteria.

## Creating a New Course Using Agile Backward Design

I teach in the Professional Writing and Rhetoric (PWR) concentration in my department, one of four possible concentration areas of the English major that students may select. In addition to several electives, students take core courses including introductions to professional writing and rhetorical theory, a practical research methods course, a studio, and a senior seminar. Students also take a 300-level special topic course; the course topic rotates each year, depending on which faculty member is teaching the course. Past topics have included writing project management, writing for civic engagement, science writing, and writing for Web 2.0.

Most recently, I taught the course as grant writing for non-profit organizations because we had had increasing interest among our students in working with non-profit organizations, and external requests for a similar course indicated that it would be attractive to students outside the major. The course was also an opportunity to use service-learning pedagogy to engage students with organizations in the community who have real funding needs. Working with our service-learning office, I lined up five partners for my students to work with during the course. Though technically the course was the annual special topic course, it was essentially a new course that had never been taught in our program and required development from scratch.

## Grant Writing: Brainstorming about the Course

Before starting my invention process, I reviewed familiar and new literature related to grant writing and working with non-profit organizations, reread the syllabus and textbook used in a graduate seminar I had taken on grant writing, and explored web resources available to non-profits related to funding issues. Then, using the brainstorming questions above, I generated a list of questions I wanted my students to be able to answer at the end of the course:

> What is grant writing in meaningful contexts?
> What is a community? How does it form, sustain, reach out, and attract members?
> Why do places like our partner organizations exist in the world, and how do they fit into our society?
> What is the difference socially and rhetorically in thinking of these community agencies as partners rather than clients?
> What rhetorical strategies and research methods can be adapted for use in writing effective grants? How do you choose an appropriate strategy?
> Who are the audiences our clients address? How do you reach an audience ethically and rhetorically?
> What role does grant writing play in the day-to-day operations of these agencies?

I also generated a more traditional list of learning goals for the course:

> Develop a repertoire of strategies and tools to assess complex rhetorical writing/design situations in order to recommend rhetorically appropriate actions (problem solving).
> Learn how to look for grants, assess partner needs, and write persuasive grant applications that fulfill both the call-for-proposal requirements and the partner's needs.
> Learn and practice research, interviewing, and writing skills in addition to concepts of visual rhetoric to support written arguments.

Learn to successfully collaborate with people with different skills
in order to get the best out of all group members and meet the
partners' rhetorical needs.

Develop planning and knowledge management practices including
project briefs, communication audits, progress reports, project
task tracking, proposals, and project evaluation.

Understand the value of participating in a community through hard
work and application of personal skills.

Articulate pre-course assumptions about service, learning, rhetoric,
and community partners and the effects of course experience on
these assumptions.

Understand the complex rhetorical positioning of community partners and their funding challenges within their communities.

This gave me a great deal to think about and helped me realize I was
initially hoping to achieve too many learning goals in one course, especially because slightly more than half of the students had no background in professional writing or rhetoric.

## Grant Writing: Articulating Epics and Stories

Based on my brainstorming, I developed two overarching epics and
several stories on which to frame the course. In this particular case, I
created one epic that encompassed all special topic courses in my program and one particular to my grant-writing course:

1. *As the required special topic course in the PWR concentration
   and a course that will attract many non-majors, the course will
   provide students with a deeper study of rhetorical theory and
   practice as well as further opportunities to develop themselves as
   rhetors.*

2. *As a course addressing an important area in professional writing, this course serves to introduce the process of persuasive grant
   writing through real service to the community so that students
   will understand the complexities of funding for non-profits and be
   able to use effective rhetorical strategies to write successful grants.*

This allowed me to focus on both the specific positioning of the course in the curriculum as well as the goals of the particular new course. For this exercise, I also chose to create stories for the second epic from a student perspective to match the user story model and to keep my students in mind:

> 2.1. *As a student interested in grant writing for non-profits, I want to understand the role of grants in the funding system for non-profits.*
>
> 2.2. *As a student interested in grant writing, I want to learn a set of rhetorical strategies that I can apply to write a persuasive and successful grant for my community partner.*
>
> 2.3. *As a student interested in grant writing, I want to be able to analyze a call for proposals to identify whether my organization qualifies, the required submission process, and key areas of the proposal I will write.*
>
> 2.4. *As a student interested in grant writing, I want to learn new strategies for successfully collaborating with both my peer team and my community partner so that we can draw on everyone's strengths to create the best proposal possible.*
>
> 2.5. *As a student interested in grant writing, I want to write a full grant so that I can practice the process.*

After creating, revising, and prioritizing my stories, I then began to create the assessment criteria for the course.

## Grant Writing: Determining Assessment Criteria for Epics

To determine assessment criteria, I broke out each story in a table and brainstormed ways students might show they have achieved that goal. After brainstorming, I applied Wiggins and McTighe's aspects of learning to ensure I was considering different types of learning in the course. Below are assessment criteria for story 2.2:

> Student can explain different basic rhetorical concepts such as the rhetorical situation; ethos, pathos, logos; the Five Canons of Rhetoric, etc.

Student can apply Aristotle's triangle to analyze the rhetorical situation of a grant proposal.

Student can conduct careful audience analyses of the community partner, the public the partner serves, and the potential funder.

Student can use invention strategies to create persuasive appeals in response to a grantor's call for proposals.

Using the epics, stories, and assessment criteria for the grant-writing course, I was able to start to formulate a loose schedule, potential content for the course, possible assignments, and heuristics for student evaluation.

## Grant Writing: Framing the Course Schedule

Because the course was a designated service-learning section, I knew that a loose but structured schedule would be more appropriate than a tight, preplanned one because projects involving outside partners can be unpredictable. And because teams would be working with different organizations, each would, to some extent, need to determine their own schedules with their partner contacts.

Table 7.4 shows a draft of my schedule mapped according to the complete list of stories I created for the class. Each sprint is associated with stories that complete the epic. While Scrum teams would not usually allow stories to run across several sprints, the learning context of the course required that overlap for optimal student learning. Based on this preliminary sprint plan, I created the loose but structured schedule I desired for the course. See the complete schedule in appendix 7.1.

Using an Agile backward design approach allowed me to create a new, experimental course that had the potential to achieve the expressed goals of special topic courses in my program's curriculum and to fulfill students' desire to serve their community through their writing. In the next section, I discuss how I used this process to revise my specialty elective course to fit new time constraints.

TABLE 7.4  Draft of grant-writing course sprints and activities

| Sprint | Stories | Activity/assignment |
|---|---|---|
| 1 | 1 | • Readings, rhetorical strategy overviews, context for course Readings about funders and non-profits, how to read CFPs, practicing professionalism (journal)<br>• Writing personal professional documents (assignment) |
| 2 | 1, 2, 3 | • Readings about full grant process and standard grant component<br>• Guest speakers from community about needs/grants (journal)<br>• Practicing a small grant (assignment) |
| 3 | 2, 3 | • Beginning major grant project with partners<br>• Readings on process and sections (journal)<br>• Drafting intros, arguments, narratives (assignment)<br>• Team evaluations (feedback) |
| 4 | 3, 4, 5 | • Continuing major grant project<br>• Readings on process and sections (journal)<br>• Drafting and revising narratives, implementation plans, budgets, benefits and outcomes statements (assignment)<br>• Team evaluations (feedback) |
| 5 | 5, 6 | • Completing full partner grant including front and end matter (assignment)<br>• Related readings (journal)<br>• Team evaluations (final feedback) |
| 6 | 7, 8 | • Readings about funders and granting process (journal)<br>• Writing fund distribution recommendations (assignment)<br>• Finalizing distribution decision as committee (assignment) |

## Revising an Existing Course Using Agile Backward Design

The process of revising a course using Agile backward design is very similar to designing a new course; most of the new work occurs in reviewing and revising course objectives as stories. Within my program, students take two or three elective courses depending on their path through the major. I have taught our 300-level publishing course four times in the last eight years, changing up the structure each time. Except for the first iteration of the course, I have used a service-learning pedagogy to introduce students to creating written and visual documents that fulfill a real need in the community. While the course usually runs for a full 14-week semester, the last iteration was scheduled during our winter term, three weeks in January during which students take one course that meets three hours a day for three weeks. Many students travel on special study-abroad experiences, while those on campus have the opportunity to immerse themselves in a topic for the month. In moving the course to winter term, I needed to redesign the expectations and structure of the course, thinking about how to use service learning while respecting the time my community partner could commit to the one-month-long project.

For this version of the course, I was lucky to be able to work with an exotic animal sanctuary, a long-term partner that I had worked with in at least four other courses. In fact, my students had created a coffee-table book several years ago, which was still being sold in the organization's gift shop. Recognizing the book was out of date, we decided to work together to revise it in the winter term course. Also recognizing the unique time constraints and the intensity of the course, we jointly decided that my primary contact at the organization for this winter term project would be a young woman now working at the organization who had graduated from my program and completed several projects with the organization as a student. She understood the winter term dynamic and, because she would be on winter break from graduate school, could promise quick responses and deep interaction with the students working on the project.

## Publishing: Brainstorming about the Course

Before starting my invention process, I reviewed syllabi, assignment sheets, student deliverables, class notes, notes to myself during the courses, and books I had used in the past iterations of the course. I also spoke with several of my colleagues about how they saw the course fitting into our curriculum and reviewed our program assessment plan to remind myself of what goals the course must meet. I wrote down the already percolating new ideas I had for the course so that I would not lose them during the (re)invention process. I then met with my former student/partner to determine what page spreads in the book would be revised or replaced so that she could set up the interview contacts and locate pictures before the students began; there simply would not be enough time for the students to do that preliminary work in this shorter timeframe. In other iterations of the course, I might not approach potential service-learning partners until after I had done this course pre-work, but this was a special situation given my existing relationship with the organization and intensity of the winter term.

Based on this work, I then adapted existing course goals and major questions from the last iteration and brainstormed possible new goals and questions, as shown in table 7.5. As you can see, many of the course goals are similar, but the major questions I wanted students to address are broader in the winter term iteration than those posed in the past. While I had based previous iterations solely on partner projects, the time constraints of the winter term would not allow that. Additionally, in my response to my post-class notes from other iterations and student course evaluations, I wanted to do more in class to explore fundamental rhetorical concepts related to both desktop publishing and publishing as a field in which my students were considering careers. These thoughts also impacted how I developed the epic and stories for the course.

## Publishing: Articulating Epics and Stories

After my invention process, I began to frame the course as an epic with associated stories, using the process described above.

> *As a 300-level elective in the program, this course serves to introduce students to theories of writing and authorship and well as practice with the rhetorical concerns inherent in the publishing process so that students can create rhetorically effective published material in different contexts and make informed decisions about the value of existing published material.*

> 1. *As a student considering publishing as a career, I want to understand the publishing process so that I can make an informed decision about a possible career after completing this course.*

**TABLE 7.5** Brainstorms for new iterations of a publishing course

| Course goals from last iteration | WT publishing course brainstorm |
| --- | --- |
| • Develop a repertoire of strategies and tools to assess complex rhetorical writing/design situations in order to recommend rhetorically appropriate actions (problem-solving). | • Understand historical and rhetorical issues surrounding print culture, including ideas about text, authorship, readership, publishing, and community. |
| • Learn and practice research, interviewing, and writing skills + concepts of visual rhetoric, graphic design, and page layout | • Develop repertoire of strategies to assess complex rhetorical situations in order to recommend rhetorically appropriate actions (problem-solving). |
| • Write/design/manage publications for REAL clients who will use publications after our semester is finished. | • Practice research, interviewing, and writing skills + concepts of visual rhetoric, graphic design, and page layout. |
| • Learn to successfully collaborate to get the best out of all group members and meet the clients' rhetorical needs. | • Write/design/manage publications for REAL clients who will use publications. |
| • Practice planning and knowledge management genres including project briefs, communication audits, progress reports, project task tracking, proposals, and project evaluation. | • Learn to successfully collaborate to maximize group member strengths and meet the clients' rhetorical needs. |
|  | • Practice planning and project management approaches, specifically Scrum. |

| Questions for students to explore in last iteration | Question for student to explore in WT iteration |
| --- | --- |
| • What is publishing in a variety of meaningful contexts? | • What is a community? What role do texts play in forming, sustaining, reaching out, and attracting members and representing the community to outsiders? |
| • What is a community? How does it form, sustain, reach out, and attract members? | • What is a text, and what is its relationship to authors and audiences? |
| • Why do places like <partner> exist in the world, and how do they fit into society? | • What/who is an author, and what is the author's relationship to text and audience? |
| • Who is the audience <partner> addresses? Should that be the audience? How do you reach the audience ethically and rhetorically? | • What/who is an audience or reader, and what is the audience's relationship to author and text? |
| • How will we know if we are doing "the right thing" for <partner>? | • What is publishing in a variety of meaningful contexts? |
| • What do we already know about professional writing and rhetoric that can guide us in our partnership? | • When can we call something "published"? |

2.  *As a student interested in publishing, I want to understand the history of publishing so that I can understand the impact of texts and technologies on our society.*
3.  *As a PWR student, I want to understand the underlying rhetorical theories of writing and publishing so that I can apply appropriate theoretical perspectives to my practical work.*
4.  *As a student interested in publishing, I want to be able to determine and carefully analyze an audience so that I can choose the most effective organization and visuals for a text.*
5.  *As a PWR student, I want to practice aspects of the publishing process (planning, drafting, editing, designing) so that I can create successful documents in my future courses and senior seminar.*

In writing these stories, I changed the student position in an attempt to understand different student perspectives. I then continued to revise and prioritize the stories until I was confident the course could meet those goals for my program and for students. For example, the first story in the list above is not directly related to the course epic, nor is it something I can realistically assess for in the course. For these reasons, I deleted that story. The other four stories were more feasible and met my course goals, so I worked with those as I moved on to determining assessment criteria.

## Publishing: Determining Assessment Criteria for Epics

Writing assessment criteria for the stories followed prioritizing the backlog. In this course, I wanted to create assessment criteria in which theory and practice were equally balanced. Here is how I articulated assessment criteria for a theory-based story and a practice-based story.

**Theory Story:** *As a PWR student, I want to understand the underlying rhetorical theories of writing and publishing so that I can apply appropriate theoretical perspectives to my practical work.*

Student can summarize the key values of oral, written, print, and online publishing cultures and discuss the impact of each on human communities.

Student can identify at least two theories of authorship and create a provisional definition of authorship.

Student can identify at least three theories of audience and articulate a personal process for identifying audiences.

Student can identify rhetorical strategies used by authors to reach readers in different rhetorical contexts.

**Practice Story:** *As a PWR student, I want to practice aspects of the publishing process (planning, drafting, editing, designing) so that I can create successful documents in my future courses and senior seminar.*

Student can articulate steps in the publishing process for both desktop and manuscript publishing.

Student can create a realistic and feasible publication plan for a document.

Student can assess final audience for document and make effective choices about content and layout.

Student can draft effective content for a document with a particular audience.

Student can edit for other students, understanding when to use substantive versus copyediting strategies.

Student understands basic page-design principles and can design a page spread in a chosen software program.

These criteria align both with the story and with the questions I brainstormed in step 1 of this process, bringing the course outcomes full circle.

## Publishing: Framing the Course Schedule

In this case, I had several previous syllabi to build on and had a good sense of the general rhythm of the course, but I had to rethink the schedule in light of my new stories and the winter term time frame. Whereas I had defined the course in 4 to 5 very loose sprints in the past, this schedule needed to be a bit tighter and somewhat more controlled. To achieve my goals and complete the stories, I created a new variation of a project I had experimented with many years ago and added a sprint for that project to the calendar in addition to the service learning project. I ultimately determined four major stories for the course and three sprints. Table 7.6 shows the sprint plan for the course.

The complete schedule for the course can be found in appendix 7.2. While I used the same process to create the special topic grant-writing course, more work occurred during the invention phases because the schedule and reality of what could be accomplished in the given timeframe was unique. I could have simply used backward design to revise the course, but using the Agile backward design process described here helped me to separate my new iteration of the course from the previous ones in my mind. I was able to draw on the past courses but not become stuck in my past thinking about the course.

Using Agile backward design process, I have found that my courses are more strategically aligned with program goals, more innovative in terms of pedagogy and student work, and better environments for engaged student learning.

TABLE 7.6  Sprint plan for winter term publishing course

| Sprint | Stories | Activity/assignment |
|---|---|---|
| 1 | 1, 2 | • Readings—history of publishing, evolution of writing/written culture (blog)<br>• Begin manuscript project |
| 2 | 1, 2 | • Readings—theories of authorship (blog)<br>• Manuscript project |
| 3 | 1, 3, 4 | • Reading—audience and readership theories, publishing industry (blog)<br>• Partner project |

## Adapting the Agile Backward Design Process in Other Contexts

The two course design examples shared above illustrate how Agile backward design can be used by individual faculty members to create and redesign personal courses. But course design happens in other contexts as well.

## Multi-section Courses

Courses are not always open to design by individual faculty members, as some courses may serve many students across the university in multiple section offerings. For example, an introductory biology course might be required of all biology majors and be an option for any student at the university looking for general studies credit. First-year writing courses are often required for every student at an institution and can be taught by a cadre of graduate students who may be new to teaching. In these cases, instructors across sections might share a single syllabus to ensure consistency.

To use the Agile backward design process in this case, invite a group of instructors to a design group charged with creating or revising the multi-section course syllabus. If the course is being revised or updated, ask individuals to use the process before the meeting to create a set of possible epics and stories based on the existing course objectives. When the group meets, they can use the initial ideas to brainstorm a set of agreed-upon stories and assessment criteria that can eventually be built into a schedule with readings, activities, and assignments to be used across the course sections.

## Curriculum (Re)Design

In the happy event that you are able to work with a team to create a curriculum for a new program, epics and stories are valuable tools that can be used to work out a structure for the courses. In this case, the program itself would be the epic and each proposed course, a story. Assessment criteria can be created for each story/course to determine which courses will best meet the program goals.

While a traditional program design structure might look like figure 7.1, a structure created using Agile backward design might look more like figure 7.2. Figure 7.2 illustrates an initial program structure that focuses on foundations and experiences for students rather than specific courses. Under the latter program structure, specific stories can be articulated for each aspect of the curriculum, and courses can be designed to achieve the epics and underlying stories of the program. This ensures that courses are created in service of the program objectives rather than serving other priorities such as faculty niche areas or being in competition with other programs, for example.

This process can also be used to redesign a curriculum or simply to determine if the existing structure aligns with current program objectives. Consider mapping the existing curriculum using models such as the those in figures 7.1 and 7.2. First, map the course hierarchy of the program. Then create a second map that identifies the structure of the curriculum based on how experiences that achieve program objectives are distributed. Using this map, you can determine if the existing courses are achieving program goals and identify places where courses must be redesigned or created to better serve students in the program.

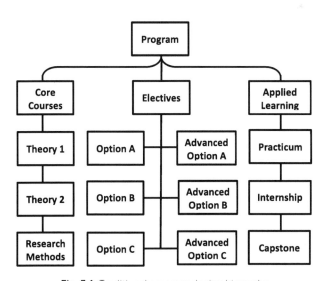

**Fig. 7.1** Traditional program design hierarchy

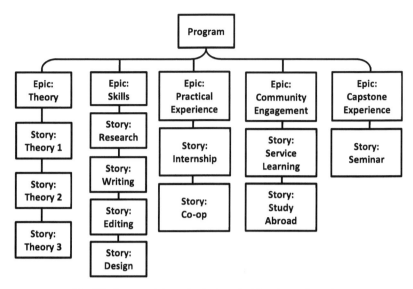

**Fig. 7.2** Program hierarchy designed with epics and stories

As noted above, the Agile backward design process is one new tool that faculty can use to rethink courses, and this process can be used in conjunction with other strategies faculty might already be using to do this work. I appreciate this process because it allows me to articulate and visualize courses in a way that can shake up my thinking and help me be more innovative in how I plan to help students achieve course learning goals. Whether you use the entire process or just a piece, the new perspective generated can be invaluable to creating a productive course.

## Wrapping Up

Thinking about your course as an epic can be a refreshing change of pace and an excellent activity for reimagining a course. In the next chapter, we will explore how to adapt the sprint model further by using it to create collaborative course projects and to reconsider your role in the class by acting as a product owner and Scrum Master for the project.

# Appendix 7.1: Complete Schedule for Grant Writing Course

| Weeks | Reading schedule and project work |
|-------|-----------------------------------|
| 1–2 | • Introduction to course and grant writing as a rhetorical skill set and genre<br>• Understanding grant funders and community needs; sample CFPs and grant application<br>• Readings: Koch intro, chapter 2, appendix; Karsh and Fox Funders Roundtable: Economic Summit, lessons 2, 3, 4, appendix 4<br>• Personal Narrative/Partner Introduction due |
| 3–4 | • Understanding the full granting process; components of standard grant applications<br>• Readings: Koch intro (review), chapters 2, 3, 4, 5; Karsh and Fox lessons 1, 5, 6, 7, appendix 2<br>• Writing a mini-grant assignment<br>• Journal 1 due<br>• Guest speakers from MERC 9.10; FAS 9.12; Conservators' Center 9.17; Positive Attitude Youth Center 9.19 |
| 5–7 | • Intro to major partner grant writing project; assigning partner groups, preliminary group activities<br>• Readings: Koch chapters 9, 10: Karsh and Fox lessons 8, 9<br>• Guest speaker from Friendship Adult Day 9.24<br>• Interpreting the CFP; understanding the need and how it matches the CFP; understanding messaging and narrative argument<br>• Drafting narratives<br>• Due: Monday—Mini-grants; Every Wednesday—journals; Week 6—team evaluations (feedback) |
| 8–11 | (Fall Break)<br>• Drafting and revising narratives, implementation plans, budgets, benefits and outcomes statements<br>• Readings: Koch chapters 11, 12, 13, 14; Karsh and Fox lessons 10, 12, 13, 14<br>• Due: Mondays (in order)—narrative draft and partner feedback on narrative, implementation plan and partner feedback on plan, budget draft and partner feedback on budget; Every Wednesday—journals; Week 9—team evaluations |
| 12–13 | • Creating front and back matter; pulling grant application together cohesively<br>• Readings: Koch chapters 8, 15, 16; Karsh and Fox lessons 15, 16, appendix 1<br>• DUE: Week 12—full draft with partner feedback; Week 13 (before Thanksgiving Break)—full grant; Every Wednesday—journals; Week 13—final team evaluations |
| 14–15 | • Read all grant proposals from peers; draft personal report recommending distribution of funds<br>• Work as group to determine actual distribution of funds (Wednesday)<br>• Final journal due last Wednesday |
| Exam | • Due: Final reflective portfolios<br>• Gathering with all community partners and announcement of grant awards |

# Appendix 7.2: Complete Schedule for Publishing

Sprint 1    January 7—Introduction to the course and the Big Questions; Connections between publishing and rhetoric; What do you want to write about for the Manuscript Project? Readings (in class)—F&M introduction; Plato, except from Phaedrus (use Ctrl+F to search for "true and false art of speaking" as your starting point; end at "utmost extent of human happiness.") BLOG POST (in class)

         January 8—Evolution of Writing and Literacy. Understanding historical and rhetorical aspects of alphabet development in ancient world; Arguments for and against literacy across early history; Impacts of Writing on humans/communities in early/medieval civilizations. Workshop: Writing your treatise (bring a black or brown fine to medium tip Sharpie). Readings (before class)—F&M chapter 2, Robinson chapter 1, Standage chapter 1. BLOG POST (before class)

Sprint 2    January 9—Origins of Print and Scribal Culture. Workshop—Treatise commenting. Readings—F&M chapter 3, <Robinson chapter 2>. BLOG POST

         January 10—Intersections between Text-Author-Reader. Workshop: Scribing treatises. Reading: Baron. BLOG POST

         January 11 (Saturday)—9am tour partner location. BLOG POST

         January 12—Illustrating your manuscripts

         January 13—Shades of Authorship. Manuscripts Due. Workshop—Reviewing your finished manuscripts. In-class paper. Readings—F&M chapter 5

Sprint 3    January 14—Authorship Theories. Workshop—reviewing partner's materials, preparing for Skype call with Kasey and for adopter interviews. Readings—Barthes; Foucault. BLOG POST

         January 15—Audience and Readers. Workshop—Skype with Kasey, make adopter contact, review/sort animal and adopter images. Reading—F&M chapter 6. BLOG POST

         January 16—Audience and Readers. Workshop—possible adopter interviews, working on spreads. Readings—Iser, Manguel. BLOG POST Pods 1 and 2.

         January 17—Audience and Readers. Workshop—possible adopter interviews, working on spreads, possibly working on Adopter Book project. Readings—Ong, Ede and Lunsford. Pods 3 and 4.

         January 21—Design Interlude. Workshop—project work. Readings—White Space chapters 1–7 and 15.

         January 22—Printing and Book Selling. Workshop—project work. Readings—F&M chapter 5, Robinson chapter 7. BLOG POST

         January 23—Text and Community. Workshop—project work. Readings—Duguid and Seely Brown, Debs or Driskall TBD. BLOG POST

         January 24 and January 27—Workshop—project wrap-ups, possible presentation to partner reps. Readings—F&M chapter 7, Standage epilogue, articles you provide. BLOG POST.

# 8

# Planning and Implementing
# Scrum-Based Group Projects

After reading this chapter, you will be able to

- Consider a group project within the course as an epic with associated learning stories
- Design a short-term or long-term Agile group project that helps students complete course stories and develop strong cooperation or collaboration skills
- Plan a lesson to teach students about the Scrum collaboration process
- Prepare to act as both product owner and Scrum Master during the group project

Portions of this chapter appeared previously in Pope-Ruark, 2014. For further perspective, see Pope-Ruark, 2015; Pope-Ruark, 2012; Pope-Ruark, Eichel, Talbott & Thornton, 2011.

A computing sciences project that gives students two months to work in Agile teams and create a mobile app that addresses some need on campus

A marketing project that requires a group of business majors to work with a community partner to assess the partner's existing marketing efforts and to create a revised marketing plan with spec work

An engineering project that asks groups of students to build an effective tool that can be used by individuals with back injuries to reach items on high shelves without raising their arms above their shoulders

A group paper for an international studies class that asks student groups to explore the most pressing political issues in a certain region

Creating group projects like these that connect students with course content and each other can be an interesting challenge. I have always used group projects in my writing courses, initially because I just assumed that's what faculty were "supposed to do." Now I use these projects because collaboration—real, sustained, authentic collaboration—is a skill that my students must practice to be successful in the future. But group projects can be frustrating for individual students (and for those grading students' work), regardless of how valuable applying content, practicing collaboration, and managing projects are for our students.

As noted in chapter 1, I initially came to Agile and Scrum because I was looking for a way to help my students develop stronger collaboration skills. But moving to Scrum helped me rethink why and how I implemented group projects of all lengths and sizes in my courses. This allowed me to create better learning environments in which my students could achieve learning goals as well as practice more authentic collaboration.

In this chapter, I introduce how to use Agile strategies to develop short- and long-term student group projects using the Scrum framework. Scrum is a natural fit for longer projects given its very origins in long-term software development projects. But even in short projects, you can introduce Agile strategies to help students self-direct their work, produce better products, and coordinate team efforts. Expanding, but not relying, on some of the concepts discussed in chapter 7, this chapter explores how to design projects for both cooperation and collaboration using an Agile model, how to teach simple Scrum techniques that students can use to manage project work, and how to act as product owner and Scrum Master during the project.

## Comparing Cooperation and Collaboration

Before we discuss Scrum-based project development in general, let's look at what we mean when we talk about collaboration and group projects. Collaboration is a buzzword today in higher education and in industry, but buzzwords can lose their meanings. Morton Hansen (2009), leading Harvard Business School collaboration researcher, defined collaboration as teams working "on a common task or provid[ing] significant help to each other" (p. 14). But noted technical communication scholar Rebecca Burnett and her colleagues recently defined collaboration more substantially as

> substantive *interactions* between and among *people* who share *goals* and exchange information as they work toward those goals in a variety of *settings* and with a variety of *tools*, either because the task size or *complexity* is too great for a single person or because the task will benefit from multiple *perspectives*. (Burnett, Cooper & Welhausen, 2013, p. 458, emphasis in original)

Collaboration is certainly a skill students will need in the workplace. Few careers will require the isolation of the traveling salesmen of yesteryear. But when it comes to group projects, especially shorter ones, is collaboration feasible? Is it possible to engender authentic collaboration like that described above by Burnett and her colleagues in only a few short weeks? And in longer projects, can students move beyond an engrained focus on individual grades to create a product that is greater than the sum of its parts?

Agile coach and author Lyssa Adkins (2010) argues that collaboration is a higher order skill that takes time to master. Groups form a cohesive identity by working together over time and developing a group culture (p. 231). Cooperation, on the other hand, undergirds collaboration. Certainly, authentic collaboration is not possible without it, but cooperation is a more fundamental ability that team members, and certainly students, must practice as well. When teams cooperate, they might commit to common goals and organize work by dividing it up, agreeing on a method of work, and determining points at which they will check progress or combine their work (p. 231). For good cooperative teams, the result is the sum of their individual but coordinated efforts (p. 231). Adkins argues that both cooperation and collaboration are necessary skills for successful Agile teams.

When designing student group projects, making this distinction between collaboration and cooperation is useful. In short group projects, faculty can help students elevate their cooperation skills, extending their existing ability to divide and conquer as well as laying groundwork for future collaboration. Longer group projects create an opportunity for students to learn skills that enable sustained focus and strategic collaboration in which they (ideally) come to trust and rely on their team members for success. Scrum-based group projects of varying lengths can encourage students to both cooperate and collaborate while also driving them to meet the learning goals of the course. The next two sections offer ideas for how to develop first short-term then long-term group project assignments designed around the Scrum process.

## Aligning a Group Project Idea with Important Course Considerations

When designing a group project, Agile or not, asking yourself the questions below can provide a foundation for your thinking about how the project will help students achieve learning goals in the course. After reviewing your course epic and stories, or your list of course goals and the content you plan to cover, jot down the ideas you likely already have for the project and then consider the following questions:

**How does the group project help students achieve course learning goals?** If you used the process outlined in chapter 7 to articulate learning goals, which stories might the project help students complete? How might the project achieve the epic of the course?

**Do you want students to cooperate or collaborate?** Both are valuable skills to practice, but it is more realistic to assume that students can truly collaborate only if the project is long enough to enable group formation and norming. Which skill is more important for your students to practice? How might you reinforce that skill when designing the assignment?

**Why is the assignment a group project rather than an individual one?** Students easily recognize when a group project could be treated as a long individual project, and they are very practical about their time and grades. In order for students to work together, they must believe they need everyone's contribution to successfully create the best possible product. Could the assignment you are imagining be completed by one overzealous student? If so, it likely will be. If students will need to cooperate or collaborate to achieve a quality project, how might the assignment be structured so that students have the flexibility to self-organize rather than follow a set of steps laid out in advance?

**How much time will the project take?** Consider your course stories or goals. Given the scope of the project you are beginning to imagine, how much time will students as novices require to complete the project successfully? How much time can you realistically dedicate in class to the project? Finding a balance between the two ensures the project meets both your goals and those of the students.

**How much control might the students have over their learning and deliverables for the project?** Providing detailed instructions for a project can be a natural instinct, especially if you have used a similar project in the past and can anticipate student questions. But an Agile project is structured so that students can self-direct their learning, to a degree. Ask yourself how you might structure the project so that students have a supportive structure but also space to develop their own process. Ask yourself what flexibility might exist in the types of deliverables students might create for the project—must they write a paper, or might it be a presentation or a video instead, for example?

**Is the group project realistic?** As the literature on client projects and service-learning attests, students often respond well to work they feel is valued beyond their own learning. A realistic context or audience can motivate students with a sense of purpose and urgency to work together effectively. Having a client or community partner is not always possible, but practical hypothetical situations or opportunities to share work publicly can be motivating as well. How might the assignment be designed to include a partner, a client, a public audience, or a realistic hypothetical context?

**Can you make it clear in the course schedule that you value the assignment as a means to meet course learning goals?** That might sound odd; of course we value the assignments we give. But we might not always connect the assignment to the work of the course clearly enough for students to see the direct impact on their learning or their lives. To students, it might seem as if assignments are external to the real work of the course, busy work rather than a valued learning experience. How might you frame the project for students to help them directly connect the project to their learning and the course content? When thinking about the timeframe and schedule for the assignment, can you build in regular in-class group time? This can help students connect the project to the work of the class, meet with their groups in a supportive environment, ask questions of you and their peers, and report back on their progress regularly, thus integrating the project into the learning experience.

Working through these questions can help you create a highly effective team project for student learning.

Agile team projects can take many sizes and shapes, and the deliverables can vary widely. Once you have carefully thought about these questions, outline the project, keeping in mind how much time the project will require to complete given its scope. The next two sections explain how I created a short cooperative project for a first-year writing course and a longer collaborative project for an upcoming iteration of my 300-level publishing course. Again, I offer these examples not as perfect illustrations but as potential inspiration for group projects within your own Agile course.

## Creating a Short Group Project with One Sprint

Short group projects that take two to three weeks in a traditional 14-week semester or two weeks in a quarter allow students to practice cooperation skills and project management, while also working toward the goals of the course. These projects can disrupt the focus on individual work and grades and shake up the routine of the course.

In my upcoming section of first-year composition, I plan to use a short group project as one of four required papers to give students practice writing papers as a team, which they will frequently be called upon to do in more advanced classes. The first-year writing course at my university is required of all first-year students, so my department runs multiple sections every semester. Though there is no common syllabus, we have a set of common objectives for the course, through which we guide students to develop

> a more sophisticated writing process, including invention, peer responding, revising, and editing, that results in a clear, effective, well-edited public piece;
> a more sophisticated understanding of the relationship between purpose, audience, and voice, and an awareness that writing expectations and conventions vary within the academy and in professional and public discourse; and
> an appreciation for the capacity of writing to change oneself and the world.

In this section of the course, I have decided to use a new approach called "Writing about Writing," sometimes abbreviated "WaW." This approach assumes the course is an introduction to writing studies as a discipline as well as a course that teaches the writing process and rhetorical strategies. So rather than writing about personal interests, students read disciplinary literature from writing studies, interrogate their own perspectives about writing, and write papers based on published research in the field. With this and the shared course objectives in mind, I created an epic for my course:

> *As the only writing course required of all first-year students at the university, this course serves to introduce students to (1) rhetorical process strategies for every stage of the writing process and (2) writing as an academic discipline so that they can successfully create effective and well-supported arguments in future academic writing situations and understand how to approach the literature of a discipline.*

From there, I created student-oriented stories to guide my course and project planning. Some of those stories include

1. *As a first-year student who will write extensively in college, I want to understand my own writing process so that I can develop planning, drafting, revising, and editing strategies to be successful in future individual and group writing situations.*
2. *As a first-year student who will read extensively in college, I want to be able to critically read, synthesize, and analyze material so that I can successfully support my written arguments.*
3. *As a first-year student who will write extensively in college, I want to learn how to assess audiences so that I can communicate in a variety of situations.*
4. *As a first-year student who will write extensively in college, I want to learn how to create well-supported arguments so that I can persuade audiences.*
5. *As a first-year student who will write extensively in college, I want to learn how to locate, evaluate, use, and cite sources so that I can craft effective arguments for particular audiences.*
6. *As a first-year student in a required writing course, I want to define what "writing" means in today's multimodal world and to understand writing as both a practice and a discipline*

*so that I can experience a new-to-me field of study and learn how to approach writing in a new area.*

Using this framework, I developed the course sprints and schedule, including three individual papers and one group assignment. I chose to create a short group project for stories 4, 5, and 6 because students will need to develop strategies for writing both individual and group papers for their future work. Though the project could have been an individual project, I chose a group project so that students could collect more literature and data to synthesize and help them complete story 6. When teams use Scrum in industry, a sprint is typically two to four weeks, so I chose to think about this group project as one three-week sprint in the course, complete with planning, daily Scrums, review, and retrospective components.

Thinking about the stories I wanted students to complete, the epic for the course, and writing activities students would have done prior to the group project, I created the following project prompt and schedule.

**Prompt.** In this course sprint, we will be discussing "multimodal writing" using chapter 4 in the WaW textbook and your own team research. The big question for the sprint is, "What does and does not constitute writing?" For example, are text messages considered writing in the same way formal letters are? Are blog posts writing in the same sense that print news articles are? What about computer code; is that writing? Or infographics, Prezi videos, or multimedia graphics? We will develop preliminary answers to these questions by reviewing relevant literature, and then you will work with a small group of peers to collect your own data about what writing is and is not in the eyes of college students. The genre of your final deliverable will be up to your group, as long as it meets the standards in the rubric. This project will help you to complete stories 4, 5, and 6 of our course epic.

**Schedule.** In my first draft of the schedule, I listed every step I thought students would walk through to complete the project. But remembering the Agile mindset that teams should self-organize their work when given helpful support, I revised the schedule (see table 8.1) to include more general steps for the week. I will work with the teams as they collect and analyze their data, think about the genre for their deliverable, and complete the actual writing, but each team might decide on a slightly different approach to the work. Leaving the schedule somewhat open gives them flexibility and control over their own learning while still working within a structured framework of support. On the assignment sheet, I will also include information about the purpose of the assignment, an explanation of why this is a team assignment, and the audience for their deliverables; this combined with the prompt and

**TABLE 8.1**  Schedule for WaW group project

|  | Reading/activities | Project Work |
|---|---|---|
| Sprint week 1, story 5 | Read: Intro to chapter 4 *WaW*; "From Pencils to Pixels"; "Instant Message and the Future of Language"; Moodle chapter on surveys<br><br>Personal writing journal, group list of questions about what writing is, group list of opinions about writing from peers | Planning, daily Scrum<br><br>Draft team charter for how to work together<br><br>Set up Scrum folder<br><br>Collect literature and new data |
| Sprint week 2, story 5, 6 | Read: "Writing, Technology, and Teens"; "Revisualizing Composition: Mapping the Writing Lives of First-Year Students"; Moodle chapter on observation; Moodle links about genres for deliverables<br><br>Reading journal: answer the end of chapter questions for both articles<br><br>Peer feedback for group members | Daily Scrum<br><br>Collect more data, synthesize literature<br><br>Write up initial plan for your deliverable, begin drafting<br><br>Develop assessment criteria as large group |
| Sprint week 3, story 4, 6 | Drafting, revising, feedback, revising, editing | Daily Scrum, review, retrospective<br><br>Drafting and finalizing deliverable for presentation |
| Sprint week 3.5 | Presentations for public review given first class of week as well as team retrospectives | |

schedule should provide enough information for students to get started and begin to ask good questions to drive their project.

For assessment criteria for the different stories, written in the style of acceptance criteria, I plan to develop a full set of criteria in conjunction with my students during the second week of the project, when they know more about what a successful deliverable might look like. I will present the students with some "starter criteria" as preliminary examples for how to create a project rubric in this style and conduct a workshop with the class to develop the complete rubric. Table 8.2 shows the starter criteria for the three stories in this project.

This project is a simple example of how one might approach designing a short team project in any class using stories, sprints, and assessment criteria. When creating a short collaborative project using this Agile approach, consider the following steps:

1. **Think about the project within the context of the course stories or objectives.** What purpose does it serve? How will it help

TABLE 8.2   Stories and sample starter criteria for short group project

| Story | Starter criterion |
| --- | --- |
| (4) As a first-year student who will write extensively in college and my future career, I want to learn how to create persuasive and well-supported arguments so that I can effectively persuade my audiences. | My team and I successfully<br>• Supported our specific claims about our definition of writing using our primary data. |
| (5) As a first-year student who will write extensively in college, I want to learn how to locate, evaluate, use, and cite sources so that I can craft effective arguments for different audiences in different contexts. | My team and I successfully<br>• Cited our four+ journal articles using appropriate APA style for both in-text citations and the references page. |
| (6) As a first-year student in a required writing course, I want to define what "writing" means in today's multimodal world and to understand writing as both a practice and a discipline so that I can experience a new-to-me field of study and learn how to approach writing in a new area. | My team and I successfully<br>• Created an inclusive definition of writing based on our primary and secondary research. |

the students achieve one to two specific stories or objectives in ways an individual project might not? Consider using Agile backward design to start the objectives first (see chapter 7).

2. **Based on the stories the course will address, articulate the project assignment in one paragraph.** Keeping the description to one paragraph forces you to provide only necessary context and key points of the assignment, thereby giving students room to ask good questions and self-organize their project work in their teams.

3. **Design the sprint.** If you will be using the planning, daily Scrum, reviews, and retrospective meetings to organize the project, create the framework for the project, including readings, activities, and project work time for students teams.

4. **Articulate preliminary assessment criteria.** If you plan to have the students contribute to the assessment criteria, create a very short list of "starter criteria" for the project that students can build on. If not, create a list of assessment criteria for each story, criteria that can be used to determine if students have completed the associated story or not through the project work.

5. **Create the final assignment sheet for the project.** Include the purpose, the stories it addresses, the sprint schedule, and the assessment criteria. See the "Writing the Assignment Sheet" section below for more suggestions on creating an Agile project description.

Students can practice Agile team communication and cooperation skills through successful short projects. In longer projects, students have the opportunity to engage in deeper collaboration and experience the entire Agile process. The next section explores how I structured the major eight-week service-learning project in my signature course, 300-level publishing.

## Creating a Long Group Project with Multiple Sprints

When feasible in a course, long-term collaborative projects have several distinct pedagogical advantages. Longer projects can provide students with opportunities to dig more deeply into a topic and to practice specific skills, especially when projects are framed within a realistic context or have an outside audience for the deliverables produced by students. Longer projects can encourage transfer of theoretical knowledge to a practical context, making the course content more tangible for students. And longer projects compel students to collaborate with their peers over a longer stretch of time, helping them to develop strategies for collaborating effectively and managing team dynamics not present in shorter group projects. Longer group projects are inherently Agile in that they can be structured in sprints and give teams flexibility to adapt as they learn more about the project.

I have used long group projects in my 300-level publishing course in its last four iterations and plan to do so again next semester. This course is an elective in the Professional Writing and Rhetoric (PWR) concentration in which I teach and counts as a writing course for all other English majors; it is also an option for fulfilling our core curriculum advanced studies requirement for non-English majors. The catalog description for the course focuses on extended collaborative writing experiences for students, and over the years, I have developed a set of objectives, now framed as stories for the course, shown here in the first column of table 8.3.

I have also aligned the projects I have developed over the years with the course stories, as shown in the second column of table 8.3. Students will spend the first four-week sprint reading about the evolution of print and digital culture and completing a project that simulates the path of a "treatise" from ancient scroll to interactive digital media. The longer-term partner project will take approximately eight weeks and will be broken down into at least three sprints with interim deliverables. Using a reflection journal set up in Google Docs and shared with only me, students will write about their activities and learning throughout the semester to draw on the benefits of writing to learn. Finally, students will create a digital portfolio to showcase their work and explore their learning about publishing, professional writing, and rhetoric over the semester.

Although this manuscript project requires students to exchange documents frequently to simulate a manuscript changing hands over

**TABLE 8.3**  Stories, tasks, and project elements for publishing course projects

| Publishing course stories | Planned projects |
|---|---|
| (1) As a PWR student, I want to understand the history of print culture, including ideas about text, authorship, readership, publishing, and community, so that I can approach my publishing work with an eye to the historical and rhetorical issues at play. | (A) manuscript project<br>(B) reflection journal |
| (2) As a PWR student, I want to develop a toolkit of strategies valuable in publishing contexts, including inquiry, writing, editing, and designing strategies so that I can be prepared to address any publication situation. | (B) reflection journal<br>(C) partner project<br>(D) course portfolio |
| (3) As a PWR student, I want to write/design/manage a publication for an actual client who will use our publications after the semester is finished so that I can experience the publication cycle. | (B) reflection journal<br>(C) partner project |
| (4) As a PWR student, I want to learn to successfully collaborate with different people with different skills (real strategic, rhetorical, compromise- and negotiation-based collaboration) so that I can get the best out of all group members and meet the clients' rhetorical needs most effectively. | (B) reflection journal<br>(C) partner project |

time, the subsequent partner project is the true collaborative experience in the course, designed to introduce students to book publishing through their creation of children's books and coffee-table books for a community partner to sell as a fundraiser. These are large book projects, as students must research the partner needs and possible book content, develop a book proposal for the partner, write the content, select and obtain the images, design the layout, edit the entire manuscript, and publish the books using a print-on-demand service. Each of these elements becomes a deliverable that smaller project sprints can be designed around. As you can see in table 8.4, though, I have planned a very loose schedule for the project that allows student teams to design their own project schedules around a few target dates.

Within this framework, I plan to use backlog planning meetings to kick off each sprint so that students are empowered to organize their work but also supported as novice publishers. Students will be asked to set up a visual backlog, either physically or electronically, that we

**TABLE 8.4**  Publishing partner project schedule

| Weeks | Sprint questions (develop the tasks) | End of sprint deliverables |
|---|---|---|
| 5–6 | What does our partner want in a publication? | Book proposals to partner* |
| | What do other publications like this look/read like? | |
| | What does a book proposal include? | |
| | How will we organize our team and the project work? | |
| 7–9 | What content will we include in our book based on partner feedback? | Full drafts to partner |
| | What visuals will we collect or design based on partner feedback? | |
| 10–11 | What is the best way to organize our content/images for reader clarity/interest? | Full revision to partner |
| | What revising and editing can we do to make the book strong, especially given partner feedback? | |
| 12 | What must we do to make sure the book is absolutely ready for publication? | Complete book ready to print |

*The partner for this course will likely be one I have worked with frequently in the past and one who is willing to interact with students throughout the project and to read proposals/drafts and provide student feedback very quickly.

can all share to keep track of progress. I plan to conduct public sprint reviews and private team retrospectives to allow students to collect feedback on both their products and their processes. In addition to this feedback, I will employ a process/product rubric at the end of each sprint, which will allow students to assess their own performances and those of their peers; I will compile that feedback with my own and offer each individual student suggestions for successful collaboration and learning goals.

This project is Agile in many ways. Students must rely on their team members throughout the process to create the best product for their community partners and their audiences. The sprints within the project give students target goals without detailed direction in how to achieve those targets, thus allowing students to self-organize and use their resources to be successful. The smaller pieces of work due at the end of each sprint allow students to make measured progress and to receive multiple types of feedback throughout the project. The Scrum meeting framework will keep students actively communicating about the project, identifying problem areas, and providing multiple opportunities to reach out for help or support. I'm looking forward to seeing my new students thrive in this project as others have in the past while still creating an environment for learning and growth.

Creating a long group project with multiple sprints follows the same backward design process discussed in the short project section above. But longer projects also require additional layers to be truly successful with Agile. Consider the following when planning a long group project, like my publishing project, using the Agile framework:

> **Frame the project for students in defined sprints.** Depending on your preference or the skill level of the students, divide the course into four or five sprints with interim products that you designate. Another option is to allow students to break the project into their own sprints after an initial planning meeting. The sprint cycle can be used to hold students accountable for creating valuable pieces of a project regularly and help them learn to better estimate tasks and manage project time. Support the group by facilitating, coaching, mentoring, and holding students to the Scrum process as necessary.
>
> **Commit to regular grooming and planning meetings for each sprint.** Because the Scrum framework is plan emergent rather than plan driven, teams must not only understand the project's big picture but also adapt their work effectively as they learn more over the course of the project. For example, the team might find a new resource that changes their perspective, collect data that does not match their initial assumptions, or receive feedback from audience members that affects the product. Holding team backlog grooming meetings at the start of each sprint allows students to revisit stories and tasks they originally planned, add and delete stories as necessary based on the last sprint, and reprioritize the backlog based on any new information. Sprint planning can immediately follow grooming.

**Require daily Scrum team meetings.** Daily Scrum meetings are *commitment* meetings rather than *progress* meetings. By regularly reporting back to the group exactly what each person has accomplished, is currently working on, and might need help with, students learn to be accountable and to hold each other to shared commitments while keeping group momentum and energy up. The daily Scrum meeting also normalizes asking for help, which can be difficult for some students. Teams can use the time at the beginning of class or team meetings to update their backlog and Scrum folder, set intermediate goals, and address any pressing challenges. Once students get comfortable with daily Scrums, I have found they become more comfortable addressing social loafing, miscommunications, and quality control with each other.

**Invest class time in reviews and retrospectives.** Just as grooming and planning meetings set the tone for a sprint, reviews and retrospectives provide the opportunity for students to demonstrate progress and reflect on process. In a review, ask students to showcase their sprint work for the class or stakeholders, including a client or community partner if available, to get useful feedback. In a retrospective, ask the teams to reflect on what went well during the last sprint and what did not, providing the opportunity for honest feedback and a new commitment to improving some aspect of the process for the next sprint. The retrospective is also an opportunity to coach students on how to interpret and apply feedback from the review. A great deal of learning can happen in these meetings as students mature in the process as collaborators.

A longer group project using the Scrum framework provides students with a structure, regular substantive feedback, and opportunities to control their own learning process while still receiving faculty and peer support. Once you have designed your Agile project, consider how to write an effective assignment sheet that conveys the project and its "agility" to the students.

## Writing the Assignment Sheet

One of the core foundations of Agile teamwork is self-organization; teams choose the work they will commit to for a sprint from the larger prioritized project backlog then decide together how they will accomplish that work. Faculty are ultimate self-organizers; we have autonomy and flexibility (generally speaking) to determine how we will organize our time to achieve goals and meet commitments across the areas of our work. Students, on the other hand, are accustomed to being told what to do in detailed assignment sheets, and they are often motivated to find out "what the professor wants" in order to get the appropriate grade rather than to meet personal or course goals. In an Agile course project, students are empowered with a process, useful tools, and responsibility to collectively organize their project work to achieve a shared goal. A strong project description and assignment sheet can help students understand their role in the project and the learning they can achieve.

Once you are satisfied that the project will help students achieve their learning goals, write the assignment sheet by providing students with enough information to understand their tasks but enough room to make their own decisions about how to work together to create the best outcomes. Consider including these elements:

**Purpose for the group project within the context of the class.** Just as a software development team needs to understand how a certain feature they are building fits into the overall application, students benefit from a clear statement of how the project fits into the work of the class. A sentence or two about the purpose of the project and a list of the course stories or goals the project will address can go a long way to helping students buy into the project. Also consider adding a sentence or two about why the project will require teamwork or collaboration so that students think early about how to work with each other effectively.

**Explanation of situation or scenario for the assignment.** Because students are typically more engaged with assignments that either have a real external audience or have realistic outcomes beyond the class, clear scenarios set the tone for the assignment. If you have a client or community partner for the project, clearly state the situation, the need, and the overall goal of the work. Otherwise, try wrapping a realistic hypothetical scenario around your project so that students see how the project might help them do something in the future.

**Information about expected activities, deliverables, and timeframe (sprints).** Scrum-based projects should be flexible, but that does not mean they are unstructured. For a shorter project, include a list of specific activities and deliverables students must complete by the end of the assignment. For a longer project, you might provide sprint end dates with defined deliverables for each sprint. Sketch out what these activities and deliverables are so students have a clear sense of what they are doing and how long each might take, even if they will have to figure out how to complete each step as a group. Consider including a brief explanation of the sprint process and Scrum meetings (planning, grooming, daily Scrum, review, retrospective) if you are integrating those into the assignment process. A handout or web resource students can reference during out-of-class meetings may be useful.

**Criteria for success.** Chapter 7 discusses how to develop a set of criteria for a course that lists specific conditions students have to meet to show they have achieved each learning outcome in a course. A similar model can be used when creating assessment criteria for a group project. State the story or stories the project addresses, and provide a set of yes/no criteria that students can use to set quality standards for their project and participation. For example, a quality criterion for the computing sciences example that begins this chapter might be "Application compiles and runs without crashing iOS." A participation criterion for the same project might be "Student on the application team successfully defended programming choices during individual code reviews." You might choose to create all of the assessment criteria or to include your students in that process as well.

In the past, when drafting group project assignment sheets, I often have had to resist the urge to create very detailed directions for my students, especially for projects that are similar to those I've used in the past. I know what questions students will likely ask, so the desire to answer those questions before they are asked is natural. But Scrum-based projects are intended to be structured, not rigid. If the project you have designed uses the Scrum process to the fullest and you are committed to letting students find their way using the process, the assignment sheet should serve as a contextual explanation rather than an instruction sheet.

Once you have created the project assignment, how do you increase the likelihood that students will thrive in the Scrum-based project environment? The next section offers some tips.

## Encouraging Collaboration and Introducing Scrum

Designing and clearly articulating the Scrum-based project is your first major step toward success. The second is implementing the project within the class context and introducing students to this different way of approaching team work. Students have natural and valid reactions toward group projects that Scrum can help them address if they buy into the process.

Students can be wary of group projects on the day they are introduced, so I have developed my own process for gaining buy-in for the new Agile strategies I ask students to implement. Because learning effective collaboration strategies is a learning goal in my courses, I typically take an entire class period to walk through these steps. This process has proved successful over the years, so I encourage you to adapt it to your context and time constraints:

1.  **Let students air the dirty laundry.** On the first day of a group project, begin with an open discussion of the benefits and challenges of working with peers. Students love sharing horror stories about past group experiences and are not often given class time to discuss those experiences as learning opportunities.

To start off the discussion, tell a few horror stories from your experience, and encourage students to tell their worst team stories, being sure to have each student summarize the project's worst characteristic (e.g., dealing with a social loafer, not having the same expectations as other group members). Keep track of the list of these bad characteristics on the board, and have a note-taker type it up for later reference.

2. **Shift the emphasis.** Once the students have created a list of "bad team" characteristics, ask them to describe their best experiences and what made that group excellent. This list goes alongside the "bad team" list so that you can compare and contrast effective and ineffective group behaviors.

3. **Create an "expected behaviors" list.** Building on these two lists, encourage students to identify the four or five most important team behaviors that they each commit to enacting during their new group project. Post the compiled lists somewhere visible so all teams have access, perhaps in a document on the course web space.

4. **Help students create their own cooperative team environment.** In industry, new Agile teams spend time getting to know each other as people and professionals by setting team rules for interaction. (See chapter 5 for team building strategies that can be used to create trust among student team members if time allows.) Once students are in project teams, ask them to build on the class behavior list and create their own team rules. What personal strengths and weaknesses does each person bring to the team? What is their regular meeting day and time? How will they communicate with each other? How will they share knowledge? What will they do if someone misses a meeting? What is the process for resolving conflict? Once the students have created their team behavior lists, have them posted to a shared space, such as a Google Doc, so that both you and the team can refer back to them as needed during the project.

After the stage has been set for the team to function well together,

5. **Have students articulate project tasks.** Ask students to carefully review the assignment and make a backlog of everything they can possibly think of that they will need to do in order to create a successful final product.

6. **Introduce the new teams to Scrum project terminology.** Once students have created a preliminary list, open a discussion about Scrum, explaining how and why the strategies will be used in this project. Then introduce Scrum language for the strategies you will use, usually backlog, stories, tasks, and possibly daily Scrum. Ask them to reassess and reorganize their preliminary lists by creating a more formalized backlog of stories and adding appropriate tasks under the stories. Help them take into account any process documents or interim deadlines required in the assignment. It's less important that they correctly identify every story or use the formal story formula than it is that they can begin to articulate parts of the process they will need to accomplish to complete a project. Walk around and provide advice and suggestions.

7. **Introduce a simple Scrum board approach using folders.** Provide each team with small sticky notes, plain manila folders, pens, and rulers.[1] Ask students to open the folder and draw three columns, making sure that the outside columns are wider than the inside column. Students label each column from left to right: Backlog, WIP (for Work in Progress), and Done. Next, have students move individual stories and tasks onto sticky notes that they put in the backlog column. Explain how they can prioritize the stories and tasks by moving them up and down the column, and show them how to choose which priority tasks to move into the WIP column. You can also discuss why the WIP column is

---

1. I prefer physical Scrum boards because people, myself included, seem to get a psychological boost from the act of physically moving tasks into the Done column. Folders work well when wall or whiteboard space is not available and are portable when students want to meet outside of class. But in different environments, software is certainly a viable option for creating the board. A Word file uploaded to Dropbox, a Google spreadsheet, or an educational version of a more formal project management software such as LeanKit can potentially serve as a virtual Scrum board.

narrower than the others, helping them to understand the value of committing to only the work activities they can finish between team meetings.

Once you have helped students set up Scrum folders, explain how you will use the folders in class to help them make consistent progress on project goals. They can adapt the folder in ways that are most useful for their team. For example, some of my teams choose to write team member names on the tasks they are responsible for in order to keep track of individual contributions. I explain that I will read their updated folders after every class, making notes about their progress and any questions I want to ask them. You might use it more formally to keep track of a participation grade, although that might defeat the spirit of self-organization for some students. But after these initial explanations, turn the project over to the students, and let them get started.

Discussing group work and project management strategies with students before a group project is a way to validate past experiences while offering new strategies for success. Basic Agile strategies give students valuable tools to self-organize work while still being supported in their learning. And Scrum can not only help students see their roles in project work differently but also help faculty play new roles in the classroom.

## Acting as Product Owner and Scrum Master

When you think of yourself in the classroom, what is your dominant role? Subject matter expert? Lecturer? Discussion leader? Co-learner? Certainly we all wear multiple hats in our courses, and even at different times within the same class meeting. Agile and Scrum are to traditional management what the learner-centered classroom is to traditional higher education; both decenter power structures and hold focused commitment to goals, collaboration, and personal/professional growth as central motivators for success. Agile practitioners also think about the role of team members and managers differently, and the roles of product owner and Scrum Master can be adapted by faculty to guide student teams.

## Product Owner

As discussed in chapter 2, in traditional industry, the product owner (PO) is the person responsible for mediating between the software development teams and the business side. The PO represents stakeholders and customers and maintains the larger project backlog. POs make sure projects are completed well, on time, and on budget and also support the team to make the appropriate decisions about how to divide and approach the work. Product owners challenge but do not "manage" the team; teams organize their own work in conjunction with the product owner and Scrum Master.

As faculty we are product owners in the sense that we are the mediators between new knowledge, useful skills, and our students. We see the larger picture of the discipline or program and design courses and projects to bring students into that work. We are responsible for challenging students to accomplish good work according to their own abilities and the standards of our programs. We as faculty also support their development by pointing to resources necessary for success. POs in industry are charged with doing whatever it takes to help the team deliver valuable products; we might then say that our job is to do whatever it takes to help our students achieve their greatest learning potential in the context of the project.

When acting as a PO in the classroom during a Scrum-based group project, keep teams on task and aware of priorities and deadlines. One of the biggest challenges of this role is resisting the tendency to manage. Encourage teams to create quality learning by delivering small pieces of work over the course of the project rather than a giant untested product at the end. Do this by including multiple points for direct feedback, both verbal and written, from a variety of sources, including you, peers, clients or partners (if applicable), and themselves through self-assessment. Groups learn by inspecting their work periodically and identifying when they need to change or adapt, with your support. Serving in this role is one way to help students take ownership of their own learning, a desired outcome of any project, large or small.

## Scrum Master

If the product owner owns the product, then the Scrum Master owns the process, as discussed in chapter 2. Scrum Masters are tasked with empowering the team with what they need to be successful on a sprint-to-sprint, day-to-day basis. They facilitate all planning, daily Scrum, review, and retrospective meetings to ensure the team is collaborating optimally and thinking clearly about commitments. When called upon, the Scrum Master helps the team reassess their process and make adjustments to improve productivity, engagement, and professional satisfaction. The Scrum Master is a team facilitator, mentor, devil's advocate, protector, and champion.

As faculty, we play all of these roles as well. We empower students to learn in the environments we create, facilitate the learning process, and help students overcome impediments as they do the work of learning. Acting as a Scrum Master can be an easy mindset shift for faculty already using learning-centered pedagogies and assuming the role of facilitator rather than project manager.

As a Scrum Master in an Agile group project, support the teams' processes. Help teams to learn to limit work in progress when working with backlogs. When teams are working independently, observe group interactions, and make suggestions to help them maximize their time and learning. When a team is stuck, help them talk through the issues and generate solutions to implement. Conduct retrospectives with teams, helping them to identify what is working well in their group process and what can be improved to ensure greater success. Support your student project teams so that they believe in themselves and are empowered to meet your high expectations for their learning.

Shifting roles in the classroom during different learning situations can be refreshing. Putting on the PO or Scrum Master hat, so to speak, is a way to break out of the usual role we play in our classrooms and offers students feedback from multiple perspectives, as POs and Scrum Masters might focus on different elements of the project deliverable and group process. These roles allow faculty to collaborate with student project teams as they work while still providing structure and guidance as needed.

## Wrapping Up

To be successful professionals and citizens, students in every discipline must learn to cooperate and collaborate effectively. By intentionally talking to students about team work and teaching helpful project management strategies such as the Scrum framework, we add value to our courses and create more opportunities for student success. Scrum is easy to learn and easy to implement in any group project that requires students to work together, and the skills they learn are immediately transferable to other contexts. And Agile provides another lens for faculty to consider how we design student learning opportunities and approach our own roles in the classroom.

Over the course of eight chapters, we have explored how Agile principles and Scrum practices can impact our approaches to many aspects of faculty work by using a lightweight framework to achieve incremental, visible progress toward meaningful goals. Agile is new to higher education, and this movement has great potential to change the way we research, serve, and teach.

In the afterword, I take a moment to imagine what Agile higher education might look like system-wide, were we to start a movement.

# Afterword

# Imagining the Agile College and University

Scrum's creator, Jeff Sutherland (2014), asks us to "imagine [an organization] that everyone thinks of as *my* [organization], where every day is a chance to get better, to do something better, to learn something new" (p. 159). This imagining is both the heart of Agile and the heart of higher education. I end this book with some "blue sky dreaming," imagining how Agile might be implemented in university contexts more broadly than discussed in this book.

What follows are simply visions of the possible, to borrow Pat Hutching's (2000) term for one variation of Scholarship of Teaching and Learning (SoTL) work (pp. 4–5). Some of the ideas presented here build on creative programs like those at the University of Maryland, Tulane, the Virginia Ball Center at Ball State University, Stanford, and the University of Minnesota Rochester. Others build on a Scrum-inspired question, What can we do right now that would produce the most value for our students and university communities? These "what if?" scenarios extend ideas in the book, and in the true Agile spirit in which this text is offered, I hope to replace these visions with realities in future iterations of this text.

**What if . . .**

## . . . important committees ran like Scrum teams?

Rather than senior leadership appointing people to an important task force, the administration sends out a call to service to the entire university and local community, asking those interested to fill out a short online survey explaining their interest and what unique perspective they would bring to the work. A diverse task force of 30 people is then formed based on the applications and meets first for a two-day, off-site retreat. The university president kicks off the retreat with a discussion of the charge, timeframe, and budget, and the remaining time is facilitated by an Agile expert, helping the members learn the Scrum process, build community spirit and collective expectations, determine the project backlog, and create small cross-functional teams to begin the highest priority backlog stories.

After completing initial background research stories, the teams focus on specific themes that emerged, conduct additional primary and secondary research for each thematic strand, and develop possible ways of addressing the issue on campus. These teams use the Scrum sprint cycle to select ideas from their backlogs, develop them, test them in real campus settings, demonstrate their findings to task force peers and the university community, and determine plans for revising and retesting ideas within their backlogs. The small teams update other task force teams on their work regularly. Thus, the resulting report, recommendations, and programs have already been tested and, in some cases, fully piloted to show proof of concept when submitted to the administration at the end of the task force's term of service.

## . . . student and faculty peer mentoring used an Agile coaching approach?

Upon arriving at the institution, students are assigned to a 0.5 credit course led by one faculty member and populated by up to nine other students of different years and majors. During the first meeting of the mentoring team, the faculty member leads all mentees in activities that help them get to know each other in terms of individual strengths; personal areas of interest in all areas of university life (academic, co-curricular, social); and work-style preferences. Then the faculty member spends some one-on-one time helping new students create goals for their college experience and an initial backlog for the semester. The faculty member also works individually with the students already in the group to assess their goals, adapt their backlogs, and set new goals for the semester. The groups meet twice a month to check in on progress toward everyone's goals, provide support, and discuss any challenges they face. Because students stay in their groups over their time in college, earning 0.5 credit hours per semester for their participation, the groups become safe spaces to share concerns and issues, with both the faculty member and other students available to offer mentoring as needed.

Similarly, faculty members are placed in or opt into peer mentoring groups based on interests and mentoring needs. Groups could be formed around interests in SoTL, work-life balance, diversity, interdisciplinary pursuits, undergraduate research, international study, or academic writing success, for example. Groups might also be formed around faculty life stages: new faculty groups with supportive mid-career peer mentors; mid- and advanced career mutual mentoring groups; faculty who identify with underrepresented populations on campus; and groups for new parents, those with young children, those caring for aging parents, etc.

The first meeting of each group is facilitated by an experienced peer mentor who offers advice on setting up group expectations, understanding mentoring strategies, building personal backlogs, and using the backlogs to guide mutual mentoring meetings. Teams also elect a Scrum Master, who receives additional training in facilitating meetings using Scrum strategies. Financially supported with a small stipend for coffee or lunch meetings, groups meet once a month to check in on personal goals, provide accountability, share success strategies and resources, and offer encouragement when a colleague requires additional support. Faculty can shift and reform groups as priorities and interests change but always have the opportunity to give and receive peer-mentoring support for their personal and professional growth.

## . . . programs were sprint- rather than semester-based?

Rather than a traditional agrarian calendar, the university uses a rolling calendar of two-month sprints within which faculty and students in functional learning teams define their own shorter cycles to achieve shared learning outcomes. Topics for these major sprints could be clearly defined for the first year of the foundational curriculum. Foundational and general education programs are developed around interdisciplinary cohorts of faculty, staff, and students and are designed to strengthen critical thinking, reading, writing, speaking, quantitative and qualitative reasoning, and collaboration skills. Program sprints incorporate flipped learning, large and small group discussions, and several of the top ten engaged learning practices—first-year seminars, learning communities, writing intensive courses, common intellectual experiences, collaborative projects and assignments, and service- or community-based learning.

As students continue into major programs, the second year would be driven by student teams and faculty mentors, and the remaining years more loosely planned in conjunction with the activities for the rest of an undergraduate's specific program of study. Program pathways can be designed by students to incorporate time off for internships or other immersive experiences that contribute to learning outcomes. Students finish the undergraduate degree in three or four years provided that they achieve the learning outcomes in the defined degree areas as determined by program faculty and are positively assessed through sprint reviews, retrospectives, written artifacts, and a comprehensive portfolio. Students must also work in conjunction with their student and faculty mentors to make sure they complete eight out of ten of the AAC&U's high impact learning practices, many of which are worked into the curriculum already. Graduate students and faculty work within these rhythms as well, and graduate degrees are awarded once agreed-upon learning objectives and primary research goals are met.

Courses within this sprint-based program structure combine specific content learning goals that relate to the previous two-month courses, embedding active practice with desired competencies through hands-on projects and service. Faculty have scaffolded learning outcomes for the courses in the programs, and faculty work with students to design a two-month learning experience that allows students to meet those objectives while maintaining substantial control over their collective learning. Courses are structured using the Scrum framework of meetings—planning, daily Scrum, reviews, and retrospectives—so that students receive regular feedback from both inside and outside the course context. The final review and retrospective is held between the student and supervising faculty, who review the student's portfolio of accomplishments for the course and jointly assess whether the student has adequately achieved the course objectives in order to move forward to the next step in the program.

## . . . research teams were housed in interdisciplinary, collaborative, Agile centers?

Rather than being housed in traditional departmental units, some large research and pedagogical projects are housed within interdisciplinary "social labs" that combine teaching, research, service, and civic action under one umbrella theme, such as food sustainability or specific healthcare or economic epidemics. Teams are assembled from faculty across areas with different methodological and ideological perspectives, students, and local stakeholders to approach the issue from a variety of angles, using the model discussed in the program section above.

Because teams are composed of experts in different fields, teams tackle the issue using diverse approaches to types of theorizing, experimenting, testing, and prototyping unique to the mission of that team. Individual and small teams still publish their work in their disciplinary journals but also share their work regularly with the university and local community through newspaper articles, newsletters, town hall meetings, and collaborative workgroups. Without traditional silos, researchers add new levels to their perspectives on problems through their interactions with others external to their disciplines, thus opening up new avenues and approaches to important social, economic, and environmental issues.

## . . . academic publishing used an Agile model?

Rather than publishers serving as the de facto gatekeepers of academic publishing, faculty and researchers reclaim the rights to their intellectual property in collaborative ways. The peer review system moves from blind review to open peer review—article drafts that are accepted for deeper consideration by faculty journal editors are posted to an open source database, and members of the research community with interest or expertise are invited to provide feedback on their pieces, responding to specific questions asked by the author(s) and a set of common questions required by the journal.

Feedback is cumulative through a commenting system so that the author can communicate directly with the commenters, who can also respond to each other in the forum. Based on one or two rounds of open feedback, the author can submit the article for publication consideration, attaching a cover letter detailing feedback received from the community and how that feedback was addressed in the revision. Editors can then make a recommendation to publish or to go through another round of peer review with more targeted reviewers closer to the article's topic area. Authors and commenters respect the intellectual property of their peers but also can form relationships and potential research partnerships through this open review portal.

The values of collaboration, focus, courage, openness, commitment, and respect underlie every relationship, decision, action, and project in the "what if?" scenarios above. According to Jeff Sutherland (2014), excellence can be achieved only when systems that value silos of knowledge and separation of efforts are replaced with systems that value people, meaningful work, and joy in making significant contributions to society or organizations—fundamental values inherent in higher education today (pp. 143, 147). Good blue sky dreaming about the future of higher education should not be hindered by practical concerns, and there are many logistical challenges to realizing the different pieces of these ideas. A vision of Agile education, like a vision of a new software product, is the starting point. From there, we build the epics, stories, and tasks needed to create that reality one building block of value at a time.

## Wrapping Up

I began this text with a discussion about what makes faculty "vital," how faculty develop work-lives that are dynamic, entrepreneurial, meaningful, and productive over the course of a career. As I mentioned in chapter 1, Canale, Herdlotz, and Wild (2013) hit the nail on the head for all faculty when they note, "The challenge is for faculty to be responsible for their professional growth and development as an ongoing, career-long quest" (p. 6). Agile, as a philosophy, aligns with this vitality quest, using as its foundation the idea that, in commitment and collaboration, we can achieve excellent work toward meaningful goals while continuing to grow personally and professionally in that pursuit. The Scrum values of focus, commitment, openness, courage, and respect support this philosophy and encourage us to make career vitality one of those most meaningful goals.

I hope that in reading this book you found strategies that will help you manage faculty work at both a day-to-day and a holistic career level as you strive to achieve your most motivating goals as well as career vitality. And I hope that you will share what you find to be valuable with peers and students who might benefit from reframing the way they think about work as well. Good luck as you pursue your own narrative of vitality and Agility.

# References

Adkins, L. (2010). *Coaching Agile Teams: A Companion for ScrumMasters, Agile Coaches, and Project Managers in Transition.* Boston: Addison Wesley.

Amabile, T. M., & Kramer, S. J. (2011, May). The power of small wins: Want to truly engage your workers? Help them to see their own progress. *Harvard Business Review* reprint. 1–12.

American Association of University Professors. (n.d.). Background facts on contingent faculty. AAUP.org. Retrieved from http://www.aaup .org/issues/contingency/background-facts

Ashmore, S., & Runyon, K. (2014). *Introduction to Agile Methods.* New York: Addison-Wesley Professional.

Austin, A. E. (2003). Creating a bridge to the future: Preparing new faculty to face changing expectations in a shifting context. *The Review of Higher Education*, 26(2), 119–44.

Baldwin, R. G., & Chang, D. A. (2006). Reinforcing our "keystone" faculty: Strategies to support faculty in the middle years of academic life. *Liberal Education*, 92(4), 28–35.

Baldwin, R., de Zure, D., Shaw, A., & Moretto, K. (2008). Mapping the terrain of mid-career faculty at a research university: Implications for faculty and academic leaders. *Change*, 40(5), 46–55.

Baldwin, R. G., Lunceford, C. J., & Vanderlinden, K. E. (2005). Faculty in the middle years: Illuminating an overlooked phase of academic life. *The Review of Higher Education*, 29(1), 97–118.

Baumeister, R. F., & Tierney, J. (2011). *Willpower: Rediscovering the Greatest Human Strength.* New York: Penguin.

Barber, N. (2013). The lure of the incomplete task: How creative endeavors pull us in. *Psychology Today*. Retrieved from https://www.psychologytoday.com/blog/the-human-beast/201301/the-lure-the-incomplete-task

Beck, K., Beedle, M., van Bennekum, A., Cockburn, A., Cunningham, W., Fowler, M., Grenning, J., . . . Thomas, D. (2001). Manifesto for Agile software development. Retrieved from http://www.agilemanifesto.org

Boice, R. (1991). New faculty as teachers. *Journal of Higher Education*, 62(2), 150–73.

Boice, R. (1992). Lessons learned about mentoring. In M. D. Sorcinelli & A. E. Austin (Eds.), *Developing New and Junior Faculty* (pp.51–61). San Francisco: Jossey-Bass.

Boice, R. (2000). *Advice for New Faculty Members*. Boston: Allyn & Bacon.

Bozeman, B., & Gaughan, M. (2011). Job satisfaction among university faculty: Individual, work, and institutional determinants. *The Journal of Higher Education*, 82(2), 154–86.

Buller, J. L. (2012). *The Essential Department Chair: A Comprehensive Desk Reference*. 2nd ed. San Francisco: Jossey-Bass.

Burke, L. (2013). A culture of great meetings. In B. Gower (Ed.), *Agile Business: A Leader's Guide to Harnessing Complexity* (pp. 118–20). Boulder, CO: Rally Software.

Burnett, R. E., Cooper, L. A., & Welhausen, C. A. (2013). What do technical communicators need to know about collaboration? In J. Johnson-Eilola & S. A. Selber (Eds.), *Solving Problems in Technical Communication* (pp. 454–78). Chicago: University of Chicago Press.

Canale, A. M., Herdklotz, C., & Wild, L. (2013). *Mid-Career Faculty Support: The Middle Years of the Academic Profession*. Rochester, NY: Faculty Career Development Services, the Wallace Center, Rochester Institute of Technology.

Cohn, M. (n.d.) Learn about the Scrum product backlog [web log post]. Retrieved from http://www.mountaingoatsoftware.com/scrum/product-backlog

Cohn, M. (2010). *Succeeding with Agile: Software Development Using Scrum*. Boston: Addison-Wesley.

Cohn, M., & Kearns, M. (2008). The chivalrous team member [Web log post]. Retrieved from http://www.mountaingoatsoftware.com/articles/the-chivalrous-team-member

Cross, J. G., & Goldenberg, E. N. (2009). *Off-track Profs: Nontenured Teachers in Higher Education*. Cambridge, MA: MIT Press.

Csikszentmihalyi, M. (2008). *Flow: The Psychology of Optimal Experience*. New York: Harper & Row.

Dankowski, M. E., Palmer, M. M., Smith, J. S., Brutkiewicz, R. R., Logio, L., & Bogdewic, S. P. (2009). Redefining faculty vitality: Synergy between satisfaction, productivity, and engagement. Paper presented at the 2009 Association of American Medical Colleges Group on Faculty Affairs Annual Conference, San Francisco, CA.

DeFelippo, A. M., & Giles Jr., D. E. (2015). Mid-career faculty and high levels of community engagement: Intentional reshaping of meaningful careers. *International Journal of Research on Service-Learning and Community Engagement*, 3(1).

Dey, E. L. (1994). Dimensions of faculty stress: A recent survey. *The Review of Higher Education*, 17(3), 305–22.

Eagan, M. K., & Garvey, J. C. (2015). Stressing out: Connecting race, gender, and stress with faculty productivity. *The Journal of Higher Education*, 86(6), 924–54.

Eddy, P. L., & Gaston-Gayles, J. L. (2008). New faculty on the block: Issues of stress and support. *Journal of Human Behavior in the Social Environment*, 17(1), 89–106.

Eisenhardt, S., Gilbert, J., Jones, M., Soled, S., & Doerger, D. (2008). New thoughts on supporting new faculty. *Academic Leader*, 24(11), 1–5.

Elliott, M. (2008). Gender differences in the causes of work and family strain among academic faculty. *Journal of Human Behavior in the Social Environment*, 17(1/2), 157–73.

Elkins, K., & Kane, L. (2015). What 11 successful people wish they had known about money in their 20s. *Business Insider*. Retrieved from http://www.businessinsider.com/successful-people-money-advice-2015–8

Fairweather, J. S. (2002). The mythologies of faculty productivity: Implications for institutional policy and decision making. *The Journal of Higher Education*, 73(1), 26–48.

Feiler, B. (2013). Agile programming—for your family [Video file]. Retrieved from https://www.ted.com/talks/bruce_feiler_agile_programming_for_your_family

Fink. L. D. (2005). A Self-Directed Guide to Designing Courses for Significant Learning. Retrieved from www.deefinkandassociates.com/GuidetoCourseDesign Aug05.pdf

Foote, M. B., & Solem, M. N. (2009). Toward better mentoring for early career faculty: Results of a study of US geographers. *International Journal of Academic Development*, 14(1), 47–58.

Fowler, M. (2005, December 13) The new methodology. Retrieved from http://martinfowler.com/articles/newMethodology.html

Fox, L. (2012). A personalized faculty peer support program: Less can be more. *Journal of Faculty Development*, 26(2), 55–61.

Gmelch, W. H., Wilke, P. K., & Lovrich, N. P. (1986). Dimensions of stress among university faculty: Factor-analytic results from a national study. *Research in Higher Education*, 24(3), 266–86.

Goldstein, I. (2014). *Scrum Shortcuts without Cutting Corners: Agile Tactics, Tools, & Tips*. Upper Saddle River, NJ: Addison-Wesley.

Goldstein, I. (2012). Choosing your Scrum team—rock stars or studio musicians? [Weblog post]. Retrieved from www.axisagile.com.au/blog/scrum-roles/choosing-your-scrum-team-rock-stars-or-studio-musicians/

Gooler, D. D. (1991). *Professorial Vitality: A Critical Issue in Higher Education*. DeKalb, IL: LEPS Press.

Gordon, V. N., Habley, W. R., & Grites, T. J. (2011). *Academic Advising: A Comprehensive Handbook*. 2nd ed. San Francisco: Jossey-Bass.

Gostick, A., & Elton, C. (2010, November 12). Four essential qualities of great teams.

Forbes.com. Retrieved from http://www.forbes.com/2010/11/12/teams-essential
-qualities-leadership-managing-engagement.html

Gower, B. ed. (2013). *Agile Business: A Leader's Guide to Harnessing Complexity.*
Boulder, CO: Rally Software.

Grappa, J. M., Austin, A. E., & Trice, A. G. (2007). *Rethinking Faculty Work: Higher
Education's Strategic Imperative.* San Francisco: Jossey-Bass.

Gray, D., Brown, S., & Macanufo, J. (2010). *Gamestorming: A Playbook for Innova-
tors, Rulebreakers, and Changemakers.* Sebastopol, CA: O'Reilly.

Greenleaf, R. K. (n.d.). What is Servant Leadership? Retrieved from https://greenleaf
.org/what-is-servant-leadership/

Griffin, K. A., Bennett, J. C., & Harris, J. (2013). Marginalizing merit?: Gender differences in Black faculty D/discourses on tenure, advancement, and professional
success. *The Review of higher Education*, 36(4), 489–512.

Hansen, M. T. (2009). *Collaboration: How Leaders Avoid the Traps, Create Unity,
and Reap Big Results.* Boston: Harvard Business Review Press.

Hardre, P. L., Cox, M., & Kollman, S. (2010). Faculty performance standards: Pat-
terns within disciplines in the research university. *Journal of Faculty Development*, 24(3), 5–14.

Hart, J. L., & Cress, C. M. (2008). Are women faculty just "worrywarts"? Accounting
for gender differences in self-reported stress. *Journal of Human Behavior in the
Social Environment*, 17(1/2), 175–93.

Hartman, B. (2012). Certified Scrum Master training course materials. Personal
copy.

Hassan, Z. (2014). *The Social Labs Revolution: A New Approach to Solving Our Most
Complex Challenges.* Berrett-Koehler.

Hess, E. D. (2013, April 28). Servant leadership: A path to high performance.
*Washington Post.* Retrieved from http://www.washingtonpost.com/business/
capitalbusiness/servant-leadership-a-path-to-high-performance/2013/04/26/
435e58b2-a7b8-11e2-8302-3c7e0ea97057_story.html

Highsmith, J. (2001). History: The Agile manifesto. Retrieved from http://www
.agilemanifesto.org/history.html

Hirshfield, L. E., & Joseph, T. D. (2012). "We need a woman, we need a black
woman": Gender, race, and identity taxation in the academy. *Gender and Education*, 24(2), 213–27.

Huston, T. A., Norman, M., & Ambrose, S. A. (2007). Expanding the discussion of
faculty vitality to include productive but disengaged senior faculty. *The Journal
of Higher Education*, 78(5), 493–522.

Hutchings, P. (2000). Opening Lines: Approaches to the Scholarship of Teaching and
Learning. Menlo Park, CA: Carnegie Publications.

Jaeger, A. J., & Eagan, M. K. (2010). Examining retention and contingent faculty use
in a state system of public higher education. *Educational Policy*, 24(4), 1–31.

Jayakumar, U. M., Howards, T. C., Allen, W. R., & Han, J. C. (2009). Racial privilege
in the professoriate: An exploration of campus climate, retention, and satisfaction. *The Journal of Higher Education*, 80(5), 538–63.

Johnson, W. B. (2007). *On Being a Mentor: A Guide for Higher Education Faculty.* New York: Lawrence Erlbaum.

Johnsrud, L. K. (2008, Summer). Faculty work: Making our research matter—more. *The Review of Higher Education*, 31(4), 489–504.

Jones, A. (2014). This simple equation could revolutionize your to-do list. *Business Insider*. Retrieved from http://www.businessinsider.com/simple-math-could-fix -your-to-do-list-2014-3

Kalivoda, P., Rogers Sorrell, G., & Simpson, R. D. (1994). Nurturing faculty vitality by matching institutional interventions with career-stage needs. *Innovative Higher Education*. 18(4), 255–72.

Kezar, A., & Sam, C. (2011). Understanding non-tenure-track faculty: New assumptions and theories for conceptualizing behavior. *American Behavioral Scientist*, 55(11), 1419–42.

Khuon, T. (n.d.). The Agile lifestyle. Retrieved from www.agilelifestyle.net

Kilby, M. (2013). Why coaching? In Gower, B. (Ed.), *Agile Business: A Leader's Guide to Harnessing Complexity* (pp. 100–102). Boulder, CO: Rally Software.

Kim, J. 3 problems with a bias for action. *Inside Higher Ed*. Retrieved from https:// www.insidehighered.com/blogs/technology-and-learning/3-problems-bias -action

Laestadius. A. (2012, June 11). Team liftoff with market of skills and competence matrix [Web log post]. Retrieved from http://blog.crisp.se/2012/11/06/ anderslaestadius/team-liftoff-with-market-of-skills-and-competence-matrix

Laursen, S., & Rocque, B. (2009). Faculty development for institutional change: Lessons from an Advance project. *Change*, 41(2), 18–26.

Levin, J. S., & Montero Hernandez, V. (2014). Divided identity: part-time faculty in public colleges and universities. *The Review of Higher Education*, 37(4), 531–57.

Lindholm, J. A. & Szelényi, K. (2008). Faculty time stress: Correlates within and across academic disciplines. *Journal of Human Behavior in the Social Environment*, 17(1/2), 19–40.

Mamiseishvili, K., & Rosser, V. J. (2011). Examining the relationship between faculty productivity and job satisfaction. *Journal of the Professoriate*, 5(2), 100–132.

Marriott, H. (2015). How to stop to do lists ruining your life. *The Guardian*. Retrieved from http://www.theguardian.com/science/2015/aug/10/how-to-stop-to -do-lists-ruining-your-life

Masicampo, E. J., & Baumeister, R. F. (2011). Consider it done!: Plan making can eliminate the cognitive effects of unfulfilled goals. *Journal of Personality and Social Psychology*, 101(4), 667–83.

McGonigal, K. (2012). *The Willpower Instinct: How Self-Control Works, Why It Matters, and What You Can Do to Get More of It.* New York: Penguin.

McTighe, J. (2011). UbD in a Nutshell. Retrieved from www.jaymctighe.com/ wordpress/wp-content/uploads/2011/04/UbD-in-a-nutshell.pdf

Meyer, R. (2015). How to make privacy policies better—in two easy steps. *The Atlantic*. Retrieved from http://www.theatlantic.com/technology/archive/2015/08/ privacy-policies-better-in-two-easy-steps-spotify-scandal/402235/

Murray, J. P. (2008). New faculty members' perceptions of the academic work life. *Journal of Human Behavior in the Social Environment,* 17(1/2), 107–28.

O'Meara, K. (2015). A career with a view: Agentic perspectives of women faculty. *The Journal of Higher Education,* 86(3), 331–59.

O'Meara, K., & Campbell, C. M. (2011) Faculty sense of agency in decisions about work and family. *The Review of Higher Education,* 34(3), 447–76.

O'Meara, K., LaPointe Terosky, A., & Neumann, A. (2008). Faculty careers and work lives: A professional growth perspective. ASHE Higher Education Report, 34(3). San Francisco: Jossey-Bass.

Nussbaum, B. (2013). *Creative Intelligence: Harnessing the Power to Create, Connect, and Inspire.* New York: HarperCollins.

Padilla, A. M. (1994). Ethnic minority scholars, research, and mentoring: Current and future issues. *Educational Researcher,* 23(4), 24–27.

Palmer, M. M., Dankowski, M. E., Smith, J. S., Brutkiewicz, R. R., & Bogdewic, S. P. (2011). Exploring changes in culture and vitality: The outcomes of faculty development. *Journal of Faculty Development,* 25(1), 21–27.

Pastore, D. L. (2013). Faculty perspectives on Baldwin and Chang's mid-career faculty development model. *Journal of Faculty Development,* 27(2), 25–32.

Pink, D. K. (2009). *Drive: The Surprising Truth about What Motivates Us.* New York: Riverhead.

Pojuan, L., Martin Crowley, V., & Trower, C. (2011). Career stage differences in pre-tenure faculty perceptions of professional and personal relationships with colleagues. *The Journal of Higher Education,* 82(3), 319–46.

Pope-Ruark, R. (2015). Introducing Agile project management strategies in technical and professional writing courses. *Journal of Business and Technical Communication,* 29(1), 112–33.

Pope-Ruark, R. (2014). A case for metis in technical and professional communication programs. *Technical Communication Quarterly,* 23(4), 323–40.

Pope-Ruark, R. (2012, October). "We Scrum every day": Using Scrum project management framework for group projects. *College Teaching,* 60(4), 164–69.

Pope-Ruark, R., Eichel, M., Talbott, S., & Thornton, K. (2011, May). Let's Scrum: How Scrum methodology encourages students to view themselves as collaborators. *Teaching and Learning Together in Higher Education.* Co-authors were Elon undergraduates at time of writing.

Prabhakaran, P. (2010, July 26). Skills for Scrum Agile teams [Web log post]. Retrieved from http://www.infoq.com/articles/skills-for-scrum-agile-teams

Riggio. R. (2013, January). Characteristics of good work team members. *Psychology Today.* Retrieved from http://www.psychologytoday.com/blog/cutting-edge -leadership/201301/characteristics-good-work-team-members

Robison, S. (2013). *The Peak-Performing Professor: A Practical Guide to Productivity and Happiness.* San Francisco: Jossey-Bass.

Roriz Filho, H. (2011, January 5). Achieving Agile leadership [Web log post]. Retrieved from http://www.scrumalliance.org/community/articles/2011/january/ achieving-agile-leadership

Rosenthal, J. T., Cogan, M. L., Marshall, R., Meiland, J. W., Wion, P. K., & Molotsky, I. F. (1994, Jan-Feb). "The work of faculty: Expectations, priorities, and rewards." *Academe*, 80(1), 35–48.

Rubin, K. S. (2013). *Essential Scrum: A Practical Guide to the Most Popular Agile Process*. Upper Saddle River, NJ: Addison-Wesley.

Saddington, P. (2011, March 29). Top 10 essential product owner characteristics [Web log post]. Retrieved from http://agilescout.com/top-10-essential-product -owner-characteristics/

Samuel, A. (2015). 5 work stresses you can alleviate with technology. *Harvard Business Review*. Retrieved from https://hbr.org/2015/08/5-work-stresses-you-can -alleviate-with-tech

Saunders, D. (2010). Agile self-development manifesto. *Discardia*. Retrieved from http://www.discardia.com/2010/07/agile-self-development-manifesto.html

Sawyer, K. (2007). *Group Genius: The Creative Power of Collaboration*. New York: Basic.

Schuster, J. H., & Finkelstein, M. J. (2006). *The American Faculty: The Restructuring of Academic Work and Careers*. Baltimore, MD: Johns Hopkins University Press.

Scrum Mastering. (2014, July 25). Scrum Master: The servant leader (3 tips) [Web log post]. Retrieved from http://scrummasteringllc.com/scrum/scrum-master -servant-leader-3-tips

Schwaber, K., & Beedle, M. (2001). *Agile Software Development with Scrum*. New York: Pearson.

Shore, B. M. (2014). *The Graduate Advisor Handbook: A Student-Centered Approach*. Chicago: University of Chicago Press.

Sinek, S. (2009). *Start with Why: How Great Leaders Inspire Everyone to Take Action*. New York: Portfolio/Penguin.

Sorcinelli, M. D. (2000). *Principles of Good Practice: Supporting Early-Career Faculty*. Washington, DC: AAHE.

Sorcinelli, M. D., & Yun, J. (2007). From mentor to mentoring networks: Mentoring in the new academy. *Change: The Magazine of Higher Learning*, 39(6), 58–61.

Stange, A., & Merdinger, J. (2014). Professional growth and renewal for mid-career faculty. *Journal of Faculty Development*, 28(3), 41–50.

Sutherland, J. (2014). Scrum: The Art of Doing Twice the Work in Half the Time. New York: Crown Business.

Sutherland, J., & Schwaber, K. (2013, July). Scrum Guide. Retrieved from http:// scrumguides.org/scrum-guide.html

Sorcinelli, M. D. (2000). *Principles of Good Practice: Supporting Early-Career Faculty*. Washington, DC: AAHE.

Takeuchi, H., & Nonaka, I. (1986, Jan-Feb). The new new product development game. *Harvard Business Review*. Retrieved from http://hbr.org/1986/01/the-new -new-product-development-game/ar/1

Trower, C. A. (2012). *Success on the Tenure Track: Five Keys to Faculty Job Satisfaction*. Baltimore, MD: Johns Hopkins University Press.

U.S. Department of Education. (n.d.). College Scorecard. Retrieved from https:// collegescorecard.ed.gov/

van den Heuval, M. (2010). Becoming an Agile Family. Retrieved from https:// scrumfamily.wordpress.com/

Waltman, J., Bergom, I., Hollenshead, C., Miller, J., & August, L. (2012). Factors contributing to job satisfaction and dissatisfaction among non-tenure-track faculty. *The Journal of Higher Education*, 83(3), 411–34.

Wenger, E. (1998) *Communities of Practice: Learning, Meaning, and Identity*. New York: University of Cambridge Press.

West, E. L. (2012). What are you doing for the rest of your life? Strategies for fostering faculty vitality and development mid-career. *Journal of Learning in Higher Education*, 8(1), 59–66.

Wiggins, G. (2005). Understanding by Design: Overview of UbD and the Design Template. Retrieved from www.grantwiggins.org/documents/UbDQuikvue1005 .pdf

Wiggins, G. P., & McTighe, J. (2005). Understanding by design. ASCD.

Yun, J. H., & Sorcinelli, M. D. (2009). When mentoring is the medium: Lessons learned from a faculty development initiative. *To Improve the Academy*, 27, 365–84.

Made in the USA
Columbia, SC
25 October 2018